FRONT TO BACK

a design agenda for urban housing

Sally Lewis

ELSEVIER

AMSTERDAM · BOSTON · HEIDELBERG · LONDON · NEW YORK · OXFORD
PARIS · SAN DIEGO · SAN FRANCISCO · SINGAPORE · SYDNEY · TOKYO

Architectural Press is an imprint of Elsevier

Architectural
Press

Architectural Press
An imprint of Elsevier
Linacre House, Jordan Hill, Oxford OX2 8DP
30 Corporate Drive, Burlington, MA 01803

British Library Cataloguing in Publication Data
A catalogue record for this book is available from the British Library

ISBN 0 7506 5179 2

For information on all Architectural Press publications visit our
website at http://books.elsevier.com/architecturalpress

Typeset by Charon Tec. Pvt. Ltd, Chennai, India
Printed and bound in Italy

Cover photography by Penny Cottee

FRONT TO BACK

Books are to be returned on or before the last date below.

a

for Brian

To offset some of the horrible carbon produced in the making of this book,
we've planted 316 healthy young trees in Whitmore Forest, England.

futurefo₂rests
for a Carbon Neutral world

Contents

Part one

Part two

Contents

Foreword

Housing is a basic human need and good design is an essential part of housing. One of the key messages in this excellent book is that although beautiful buildings enrich our lives, they do not exist in isolation. Key to successful urban planning is the space between buildings – delivering high calibre, well-designed public space – is the most important challenge facing our cities today.

Design is about giving order, scale and beauty to the buildings and the space between them. The book celebrates some excellent examples of good sustainable development that meet contemporary needs – in Barcelona or Amsterdam for instance. Sally's book brings together some of the best urban housing to be found in Britain and abroad – an impressive collection of work that sets a benchmark for urban housing designers worldwide.

Richard Rogers
Richard Rogers Partnership

Preface

What makes a great residential neighbourhood? I happen to live in one; tight, late Victorian, grid, generously proportioned terraced houses with a scattering of ground floor retail uses and a network of local parks. The key routes converge on a small neighbourhood centre before giving way to a succession of larger apartment blocks, making good use of the wonderful views from the hillside leading up to Wimbledon Common. At the heart of the neighbourhood are some very sound design principles. A Victorian area works because the tight continuous frontages give a strong sense of community and communal living. The apartment block areas get away with a less formal urban structure because of the quality of spaces in-between and the proliferation of trees and other greenery. On the hillside, a number of now pre-eminent architects cut their teeth, including Sir Terry Farrell. Although their designs were certainly innovative in their day, they also abided by the principles of good urban design.

The case studies presented in this book are all unique but all share the same essential ingredients for success, excellence in spatial planning, prioritisation of public spaces, selfless architecture and attention to detail. Each of these neighbourhoods was designed to last, built on true sustainable principles, combined economic, social and environmental values. Each of the neighbourhoods also flowed from a clear set of community values that respected the context without slavishly imitating the past.

The sad fact is that, at present, there are very few examples, in the UK at least, of great contemporary housing, particularly on a significant scale. The Building for Life standard, which seeks to capture great development, has so far only identified some 20–25 schemes that hit the mark on the key indicators of good urban design, good architecture and good public spaces. If the ingredients are clear, one wonders whether the recipe is too difficult to follow, but then that cannot be the case. If the Georgians could do it, and the Victorians could do it, and the Garden City movement could do it, then there is no reason why we cannot achieve the same success at the start of the 21st century. It simply needs the application of client commitment, the involvement of a skilled design team, a realistic budget and good project management.

I hope that the material contained in this book will inspire housing providers to no longer settle for a lowest common denominator solution, but to achieve places of lasting worth.

Jon Rouse
Chief Executive, The Housing Corporation

Acknowledgements

My particular thanks to Martin Crookston, Randall Thomas and Patrick Hammill for their valuable and expert contributions to this book.

I am very grateful to Penny Cottee and Jason Stewart for the cover photography and design, and to Jaquie Conway for her graphic design inputs.

Thanks to everyone at Elsevier for their kind help, especially Catharine Steers.

And, thanks most of all to Brian Cooper, for inspiration, for helping me keep my bearings, and for his wonderful way with words.

Sally Lewis

Sally Lewis trained and practised as an architect in South Africa, and has over 10 years' international experience in urban development. In 1999 she moved to the UK to complete a Masters degree in urban design. She is currently head of urban design for a commercial practice of architects in central London.

Martin Crookston, Llewelyn Davies

Martin Crookston is a Director of Llewelyn-Davies Planning in London. His projects bring together urban design skills and the understanding and analysis of local communities and housing markets, connecting them into the issues of the wider economy. As a member of the Richard Rogers Urban Task Force, Martin is frequently invited to speak and advise on issues of urban quality and management associated with the 'Urban Renaissance' objectives of the Blair government in the UK.

Randall Thomas, Max Fordham LLP

Randall Thomas is a partner of Max Fordham LLP and has over twenty years of experience in an environmental approach to buildings and cities. He is Visiting Professor of Architectural Science at Kingston University and teaches sustainable urban design at the Architectural Association.

Patrick Hammill, Levitt Bernstein

Working with residents to design new futures for inner city housing estates and failed neighbourhoods, Patrick has built up an understanding of urban design strategies that have failed, both physically and socially, and those that have succeeded. Actively involving residents in design development, and establishing their priorities is a key element of Levitt Bernstein's approach to securing the positive contribution that those who live and work in an area can play, sharing their aspirations to create new, well-designed, and sustainable neighbourhoods.

Beyond six rivers and three mountain ranges rises Zora, a city that no one, having seen it, can forget. But not because, like other memorable cities, it leaves an unusual image in your recollections. Zora has the quality of remaining in your memory, point by point, in its succession of streets, of houses along the streets, and of doors and windows in the houses, though nothing in them possesses a special beauty or rarity. Zora's secret lies in the way your gaze runs over patterns following one another as in a musical score where not a note can be altered or displaced.

Italo Calvino
Invisible Cities

Introduction

Back to front

Imagine buildings that exist in isolation – you can't, they don't. Even the house on the perfect greenfield site with no other built form in sight has a context. Yet we do imagine buildings like this. And, whilst the greenfield building is more likely to be photographed with the trees and lawn, the infill city site is likely to be photographed with the adjacent buildings, the buildings across the street, even the street itself, all carefully screened out.

This way of viewing, however, neglects to see how the fronts, backs and even the sides of a building relate to their neighbouring spaces. And as buildings are always next to, forming, framing, enclosing, lining some kind of space, whether public or private, hard or soft, busy or quiet, without an idea of context how can we begin to get the backs and fronts in the right place? How, if we look at buildings instead of places, can we begin to make sure they aren't back to front?

This book presents an agenda of design issues for housing, which can be used as a checklist, a method for communicating a design, and most importantly demonstrates a design approach that ensures we do not get our decision-making process the wrong way round. It also presents a series of case studies, each with its own design agenda and its own set of problems and chances. They show how the rules can only go so far – real projects on real sites have a richness and complexity that are a result of a fine balance between compromise and opportunity. The selected case studies are varied in scale, expression and context, but all respond and contribute positively to their immediate environment, and all have a specific issue or design challenge that can be a lesson for future projects.

The approach here is different to other books on housing because it is about lessons from practitioners in different locales reacting to the business of housing and housing architecture in a holistic way. Though the main focus here is on the design process for developing good housing and places, before we can talk about design issues and projects, we need to root our discussion in a frame of reference – a series of themes which are expanded upon in the next four chapters. Of course, this book does not begin to address all the themes and issues associated with housing, and in many cases the themes will overlap with each other. With a subject as broad and complex as housing, it is inevitable that issues will be discussed under more than one heading, especially if good place-making is a key theme.

Looks aren't everything

So, what makes a good place? To answer this, housing needs to be described not in terms of what it is, but in terms of what it creates: it is not about houses but the places housing makes; it is not about visual appeal alone but how buildings and spaces perform together; it is not a series of icons but rather a complex and cohesive interplay of form, space and social dynamics. Good places are about how good housing lives on and absorbs individuality, how people live in them and, how they are sustained.

In essence, form, space and social dynamics perform a dance in mediating between and creating places. To create a well-loved place that looks and feels right, this dance needs to be well choreographed.

Homes not houses

Although this book talks about housing, it must not be forgotten that what we are really talking about is homes. Today, buildings have become more important than places. With so much focus on housing provision, projects are becoming more about iconic gestures or novel ideas than place-making. Whilst innovation is certainly a priority in developing housing models, it should not be to the exclusion of creating neighbourly places. If we are talking about the provision of homes, they deserve to be more than just immediate space, more than the number of rooms in a house or apartment. Homes should be about what is next door; above; below; across the street; where is the sun; where are the shops; where is the bus stop; is there a choice; can I walk a different way?

Urban design

It is often difficult to see the bricks for the buildings. Or, conversely, to see the whole environment for the individual buildings and spaces. But urban housing needs to get beyond these issues of scale: every level of detail needs to be considered. A good first step is to see the interests of design, architecture, landscape and art as mutually inclusive, and urban design as the glue that binds it all into a well-loved place.

Housing needs to be seen as an urban issue rather than an architectural one, and urban design as its vehicle for a holistic approach. Housing is often about cities and cities are often about housing. If you are talking about urban design you are usually talking about something with housing in it, and the 'rules' for housing are in the most part the same as for any urban buildings and spaces. Good housing, however, should not exclude good architecture. Indeed, good urbanism demands well-accomplished design at every level. Chapter 1 looks at the broad principles of urban design as a good starting point for our design agenda, and how a design-led approach relies on all interest groups working together.

Sustainability

Sustainability encompasses every aspect of quality in housing, not just environmental longevity. For a community to accept and continue to accept its housing, the housing needs to offer a quality environment, which is coherent, and dignified. If housing is not of a high quality, it will not be appreciated, and if it is not appreciated how can it be sustained?

But what does quality mean in this context? In sustainability terms, quality describes every aspect of housing – from designers' attitudes, community ownership, form and space, all the way to the materials, colours and textures of a place, to the way it breathes, the way it stays alive and remains an attractive place to live. A street network is as important as the texture of a ground floor wall or threshold. A pleasant walk home is as important as the immediacy of things that are touched in everyday life.

Sustainability is an inevitable and overriding theme throughout this book. This is because sustainability is so central to good place-making. So, although housing accounts for a large percentage of CO_2 produced in cities, a design approach for housing that works towards environmental longevity should place equal emphasis on the need for these places to be attractive and well loved. Chapter 2 sets out the measures we can take to make our housing projects more energy efficient and ecologically sensitive without compromising the places, indeed how to ensure that they work together to make better places.

Engagement

Engaging with the community for the long term is a key aspect of designing and delivering good homes and places that are sustainable. This means effective interaction between the client, users and the wider community in the design process. Chapter 3 focuses on this critical dimension of housing provision, with particular emphasis on how housing projects live on, once the designers leave. Later in the book, discussions about the design agenda will reveal how important it is to communicate to users those design issues which have a bigger and longer-lasting impact. This in spite of the fact that many users are only concerned about what their own house might look like!

The way we live

Communication of design issues requires a clear understanding of the complex interactions between our social and spatial worlds. After all, the physical form of urban environments does not exist in isolation. People influence and are influenced by their environment. Environments therefore can be more than a stage for people to play out the complex and interrelated activities of life: they can enrich these activities and people's experience of them.

By looking at housing beyond the realm of architecture and the physicality of buildings, home environments, which increase people's enjoyment of them, can be created. Essentially, it is the relationships between the physical and social worlds that mould our environments. We are surrounded by this fact: cities are unavoidable spatial expressions of our social lives.

Housing has traditionally been an important element in the structure and diversity of cities. Even in 1516, Thomas More's Utopian vision for society focused on housing as an essential element for a better way of life:

> The streets are well laid out both for traffic and protection against the winds. The buildings, which are far from mean, are set together in a long row, continuous through the blocks and faced by a corresponding one. The house fronts of the respective blocks are divided by an avenue twenty feet broad. On the rear of the houses, through the whole length of the block, lies a broad garden enclosed on all sides by the backs of the blocks. Every home has not only a door into the street but a back door into the garden.
>
> (More, 1965)

Today, housing continues to be recognised as an important contributor to the vitality of urban environments, especially with the increased support for mixed-use development. Indeed, urban environments that do not include housing are often perceived to be 'dead' at certain times of the day or night. What's more, many people reference the city in terms of their homes and immediate environments. This means that the design process needs to create a good living environment by responding to social needs and aspirations. Chapter 4 has a look at what some of these social needs might be, which values are commonly upheld by designers and users alike, and sustainability emerges as a central theme. It also suggests a series of socio-spatial qualities that reflect the relationships between social issues and physical form. These socio-spatial qualities then become a very important dimension of the design agenda in the second part of the book.

A word about style

A discussion of architectural treatment or style is not central to this discussion, although where relevant to urban performance this is raised in the case studies.

Style and expression are of course important, but this book is about focusing on the issues that are important for making good places, which do not depend on style. Good design despite style is the key.

Of course, it is likely that a scheme which performs well in terms of style will be more appreciated than a building with less than spectacular architecture but which performs well on an urban level. Good urban design and good architecture are, after all, not mutually exclusive. In fact, if all decisions are made in terms of their place-making potential rather than being packaged into 'urban design' or 'architecture', a more coherent result will always emerge. The case studies in this book, whilst fine examples of contemporary architecture, have been chosen to illustrate good place-making through exemplary urban design and architecture.

One last point about style. When talking about place-making, it is acceptable to limit options about the way buildings and spaces relate to each other in order to create safe and attractive places. It is, however, less reasonable to be deterministic about the style and architectural expression. Too much prescription leads to sterility and a lack of variety and 'quirk' that makes our most appreciated places what they are. On the other hand, some of our most appreciated places have a rigour in their spatial framework that, although invisible, is skilfully coherent. The challenge, as with all design issues, is to strike the right balance (and make it look easy).

To conclude

This book is about designing good housing and making good places using a design agenda. It is divided into two major parts: the first sets out some key concepts and themes as a frame of reference, and the second presents the 'design agenda' and a selection of case studies. Finally the conclusion, 'Front to Back', draws out the more challenging design issues faced by the various case studies, and begins to establish where lessons may be learnt.

Hopefully, by approaching housing using a design agenda, more places will be built the right way round. Not back to front.

Part One

Part One

The urban design agenda

Martin Crookston

Director, Llewelyn Davies Planning, London and Newcastle
Member, English Urban Task Force 1998–2000

A rediscovery

All over the Western world, there is a rediscovery of the role and potential of cities, as the vital locations at the heart of economy and society. There are signs of change: of new confidence in cities and towns, and renewed appreciation of urban living. This is starting to provide a new context for excellent housing design and for the urban design of which it must be a part. Housing is an urban issue rather than an architectural one, to be addressed at every level of detail and at every scale. We cannot talk about housing without talking about urban design, and this chapter presents a broader urban design context to the design agenda in the second part of this book.

A design-led approach

Just as we recognise and expect quality in other aspects of our lives, we should be insisting on quality in the places and spaces we experience. The quality of urban life, especially in high-density neighbourhoods, depends to a large extent on good design. Without good design, we will not create the quality that will endure. We can provide jobs in new schemes, or homes in new developments; but if they are not well designed they will not stand the test of time, and once they are not the newest offer, in the most recently opened-up location, they will lose their shine.

What and who is involved in 'Urban Design'?

Urban design, and the housing which forms such a large part of our urban environment, is not just about buildings. It is also not just about what things look like, or about new developments. It is about the spaces between the buildings, the streets, the parks and the public facilities, the way new fits with old, and how all these dimensions work together to make a place.

It is therefore not just for architects: *we are all urban designers*, if we affect the built environment and the public realm that we all share – whether we are architects, planners, surveyors, engineers, developers, or even lawyers. And design is not just for designers. Chapter 3 looks at the importance of dialogue between designers and the 'users' or client, who hold the knowledge of how a place works.

The commitment to dialogue also extends to professionals. Urban design involves joint working, exploring, and decision-making with all stakeholders and therefore requires a full range of professional skills to be involved at every stage. The team members need to test and challenge each other, with the aim of producing a cohesive product to which everybody, including the 'user' or community, is committed.

'Deconstructing' design

We can use our own experience and understanding of places to help us think about what it is that 'works' about a place, what it is that we like, what it is that we define as high quality and good design. As lay people, we can go to a place and rapidly judge whether or not it has that quality and enjoyability that makes it successful (and we do this just as much when we are on holiday as we do when we have the 'professional judgement' filter switched on).

Even today, we know what works, what is 'liveable', 'high quality', 'well-designed'. We recognise it in so many places, for example:

— in London's stylish Georgian Canonbury or comfortable Edwardian Ealing;
— in provincial Newcastle's Jesmond – a high value Victorian inner suburb;
— in the skilled interweaving of apartments and city parks in the redeveloped quarter of Bercy in Paris;
— in Freiburg's new suburbs of Vauban and Rieselfeld – confidently marrying variety and harmony in an environmentally sustainable way.

Of course, some of the elements of the successful mix will be purely social or economic. But some of them *will* be to do with its physical organisation: its form, its layout, its functioning, its appearance – in a word, its design.

Typical street in Jesmond, Newcastle

Parc de Bercy housing and public park

From that relatively non-expert, 'as-experienced', starting point, one can then use the technical skills of urban design to deconstruct some of the elements. We can analyse a place in terms of its:

- *Site and setting, context and character*: A town or neighbourhood that we like has a sense of place. It draws on where and what it is, and on the way in which the forms of the buildings, and the spaces between them, play off their setting. Britain's best example is probably Edinburgh; Europe's must be Prague. The Scottish capital has a unique natural setting: the middle ages, and the 17th, 18th, and 19th centuries each added elements. The result is a popular, multi-purpose city of beauty and style, with a robust, and long-enduring form and fabric; a location for many different activities, and with a wide mixture of housing forms and tenures. Not everywhere can be an Edinburgh; but everywhere has the potential to be itself, and for designers to respect its site, its setting, and its character.

- *Public realm*: The public realm is much more than the green space of formal parks – for which English cities, for example, are rightly well known. Where the English are perhaps less comfortable is in creating and maintaining the smaller pieces of the public domain – the tiny public spaces (small squares or 'placettes') which make it a series of successive delights to walk through Venice or Prague. Successful public realm comes from the designers being comfortable with the space between buildings – even when these buildings are good architecture, the space between is as important.

- *Fineness of grain*: Often, a key to a town feeling liveable, friendly and fun, is its 'grain' or block size. Small building plots and short blocks allow frequent linkages. They generate a flexible grid and pedestrians can choose varied and interesting routes. Grids allow routes to lead somewhere, rather than have dead-ends; they provide multiple frontages for sales, views, and access. Jane Jacobs made small and varied blocks one of the key elements of what was successful about New York, and especially Manhattan, when she was analysing *The Death and Life of Great American Cities*'. Yet this grid does not have to be rectangular. Far from it: look at the mediaeval street patterns – from Delft to Salisbury to Siena: twisty and apparently irregular, but still grid networks. Fineness of grain in the plots within the blocks also generates variety in building form and expression.

- *Transport systems*: Linkage is of course about more than movement on foot. For towns and cities to work well, they have to provide good connections of all kinds, and public transport is a fundamental dimension of urban living. British towns show the results of a long, and ultimately fruitless, struggle to cope with unlimited car use. Yet better practice exists, all over continental Europe. Freiburg, for example, has intelligently and successfully balanced pedestrian priority with limited car access,

The grid network and small blocks at Bo01 in Malmo encourage pedestrian movement (see Chapter 8)

high-quality paving and landscaping, and direct tram penetration. A particularly difficult dimension of these movement issues is in relation to parking. Here, the targets of good design are to provide the parking that is necessary in a well-integrated way; remembering that the aim is to move people, not cars. Parking should be part of the solution, not the objective.

Shared surface in Freiburg, Germany

- *Intensity (or density)*: A vital element in the successful place, and a very important one, is intensity – a word perhaps preferable to 'density', which is a label often loaded with the emotional overtones of high rise, overcrowding and poverty. However, *intensity* is a serious point. The towns that we like, the ones we think 'work', are quite intensive in the way they use land, with the close succession of activities one after another, and the compactness and convenience that they offer. Convenient transport (bus, metro, and rail), variety, and accessibility of shops and services, private and public spaces are all interwoven. Acceptable popular places, 'places of choice', can be built at many different densities. Good design is the key to avoiding problems, rather than rigidly applied density standards. It is becoming increasingly accepted that more housing can indeed be created by skilled designers, in an attractive and acceptable way.

- *Mixing activities and tenures*: Another key ingredient. Liveable towns and cities are not a series of single-use zones. And the mix can occur both horizontally and vertically. 'Living over the shop' should be re-introduced into our housing projects where appropriate. Similarly, 'mix' should mean interweaving housing for all sorts of people, not breaking them down into one-class ghettos, whether upper or lower class. In recent housing schemes in Amsterdam, Den Haag, and Rotterdam it is impossible to tell who is buying, who is renting privately, who is a municipal tenant; the urban quality is good for everyone. Similarly, a mix of dwelling types accommodating a variety of family structures adds to the richness of a neighbourhood.

Iroko housing, Coin Street, London, with retail unit on the ground floor

- *The architecture itself:* This is difficult to assess, in some ways, because of the danger of arguments about style and appearance. Georgian London – and come to that brownstone Manhattan – shows how varied and subtle the choices can be, within the apparently restricted range of forms. We do not have to copy this, but we can learn from it, and from good modern practice in Holland for example, which contains some of the same thinking without aping the forms.

9

Terrace housing, Borneo Island, Amsterdam

Reconstructing as principles

We can, then, analyse and 'reconstruct' the good characteristics that people instinctively recognise. There are certain basic rules of composition and urban form which lend themselves to civilised urban living. We can identify them. We can use them to think about what works and does not work. We can draw principles from them, for better future practice.

To provide a set of ground-rules, the Rogers Urban Task Force led by Richard Rogers drew out a set of basic principles for urban design. They were:

- **Respecting the site and setting**: Designers must design from a basis of understanding, and resist the temptation to import standard solutions.

- **Respecting context and character**: This does not mean an insistence on slavish reproduction of the adjoining existing forms, but it does mean understanding and respecting the vernacular and the local.

- **Priority to the public realm**: This is vital – there must be a hierarchy of spaces, and the buildings around them must relate to those spaces; otherwise we just get the 'space left over after planning' (SLOAP).

- **Ensuring linkage and 'fine grain'**: Layouts must work to make walking easy. This can be done by design in new development; and it can be done in existing places too, by making easier routes on foot; in both cases the aim is to rebalance the place, as it is experienced and used by those on foot (or cycle) and those in a car.

- **Using land efficiently**: Designers should be looking to create and encourage intensity of activity, use and form; they should relate it logically to transport and services, with the highest intensity at the most accessible places, by all transport modes; and using this logic, they can help planners and local politicians to stop panicking about density.

- **Mixing activities**: Development can be based on accepting the co-existence of most modern activities, and we can often design out the problems that might arise; but we should be looking for genuine interactions, not a tokenistic 'mix' of uses with no real connections.

- **Mixing tenures**: The lessons of the past stress how important it is to avoid single-tenure neighbourhoods, and to build in flexibility at block, street, and neighbourhood levels.

- **Building durably**: Designs at both block level and for individual buildings will tend to be more durable if they follow adaptable flexible models – we can learn, for example, from the Georgian past in England, or modern Dutch practice.

- **Building to high quality**: They should be durable in a second sense, too – built to last, not a one-shot 30-year life.

- **Respect the environmental stock**: All development has some environmental impact: layouts and designs must minimise that impact, and maximise the sustainability potential.

The Task Force report argued that these principles, and this approach, form a vital part of re-establishing healthy lively cities at the core of our society and economy. They have been endorsed in subsequent government guidance in the UK, and are now widely accepted as a basis for integrating good urban design principles into planning and architectural practice.

These principles are embedded in and depend on a number of broader planning and sustainability initiatives or aspirations.

- The creation of socially mixed and inclusive neighbourhoods

- The provision of excellent local services and facilities that meet a range of needs

- The provision of quality public transport services

- Provision of long-term management and maintenance strategies for projects and neighbourhoods

- Engaging local communities

- Having a vision: new development should be a catalyst for regeneration.

And as designers, we need to:

- insist on quality, insist on design

- work together, as fellow professionals

- learn from good practice.

Successful urban design needs to bring together the client, the designers, the users, the wider community, and a collective vision if we are to achieve the sustainable places that we all desire. Chapter 2 looks at the 'sustainability agenda' for housing, with particular emphasis on the measures designers can take to control the environmental impact and energy efficiency of our urban housing developments. These measures can further enrich the sense of place and quality of our urban environments.

2

The sustainability agenda

Randall Thomas
Max Fordham LLP

Introduction

Picture a world of sustainable housing. Is it clear to you? Solar panels on the roof? A wind turbine in the garden? What makes housing sustainable? And would you want to live in it? Put it the other way. You like where you live now but surmise (probably correctly) that it is not sustainable. So why isn't it? And could someone create something like it that is sustainable?

Contrary to what we read sustainability is not about a triple bottom line, which uses the terminology of an accounting balance sheet and implies that we are merely statistics. It is more about combining the poetic and the material, the qualitative and the quantitative, the imaginative and the functional to create a quality environment for us now and in the future. And it is perhaps best represented by a rich tapestry that weaves strands from four major elements: design (aesthetics, architecture, a sense of place…), environmental concerns, economics and consideration for the individual and society. Ultimately, it is the quality of individual lives that counts, we need to try to re-situate ourselves in (what remains of) the natural environment.

A very simple test for designers of sustainable homes is whether they would want to live there themselves. This question is often answered at 'ground level'. Does the area feel safe, clean, comfortable, prosperous, varied and interesting? Does it look attractive?

Are there spaces for play around? Are there parks? Are there good schools and other facilities in the area? We need to think about the overall quality of the places that we are creating.

The second part of this book focuses on the design issues that are important for creating well-loved places. There should be nothing in a sustainable approach which is at odds with good place-making. Indeed, such an approach should contribute to the richness, variety and diversity of our communities and cities.

Region and site

Imagine yourself in the air, let us say 5 miles high. You can see a city and its region. The topography may give you an idea of how the wind and water flow over the area. You will have a view of open spaces, fields and parks and you may be able to infer something about the biodiversity there. Your vantage point is a bit like that of the sun, and you can see which windows light is likely to shine into, and which surfaces the sun's energy is most likely to reach. You can also see the main movement routes and if you look very closely you may be able to see how waste is dealt with – is that waste lorry to your left heading towards a landfill site conveniently located in your region?

All of this should indicate a way of thinking about the very close links between region and site. Housing needs to start with this broad vision.

Site planning

Now let us approach the site. Our approach should be to use all of its resources. If we look below the surface we have the mass of the earth, and we may have water, and we can use the temperature differences between earth and air to help heat and cool our homes. From the above ground we can view everything we see, both the buildings and the spaces in between them, as a series of potentially active surfaces which can be used to collect and channel energy and materials as well as fulfil the traditional more poetic roles such as a walk through the neighbourhood.

These active surfaces are shown in the illustration. The building surfaces could be well suited for solar energy, particularly the roofs. And the spaces around and above the buildings could be appropriate for wind energy. The Manchester competition scheme discussed below uses energy in these ways.

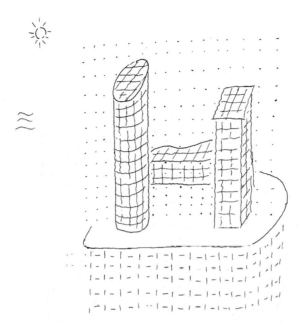

∴ ACTIVE SURFACES (POTENTIALLY) BETWEEN BUILDINGS
Ⅱ BUILDING SURFACE
GROUND

Active surfaces

Urban form

Sustainable urban forms need to find the right balance between a number of competing factors.

Items which tend to set buildings apart include:

- *Light:* light needs to be let into buildings abundantly for a feeling of well-being and to reduce the need for artificial lighting.

- *Solar energy:* roofs and, to a much lesser extent, south-facing walls should be arranged so that solar energy can be used by solar thermal panels and photovoltaic panels to produce electricity.

- *Ventilation:* it tends to be easier to naturally ventilate buildings which are spaced apart.

Factors which tend to bring buildings together include:

- *Heat loss:* denser forms have lower heat losses.

- *Exposure:* more compact forms present less exposed surface to the sun and so are advantageous where summer comfort is important (as say in traditional housing throughout the Mediterranean).

- *Heating:* more compact forms facilitate the use of community heating with combined heat and power (CHP).

- *Recycling:* more compact forms facilitate the use of water recycling schemes and waste recycling facilities.

Predicting how urban form may evolve at this early stage in the development of sustainable communities is not easy. But we can be optimistic that a fairly wide range of building/space relationships will prove capable of contributing positively to the environment. There is ample scope for innovation in finding forms that are appropriate for both environmental sustainability and good place-making.

In developing a competition entry for a sustainable community in Angel Fields, Manchester, a team of designers (Richard Partington, MacCormac Jamieson Prichard, Luke Engleback, Max Fordham LLP) I worked with came up with the following approach to urban form:

Our goals were a lively, varied, sociable space with a positive relationship to its physical and biological environment, and a place where we ourselves would like to live. The first physical manifestation of this was a series of undulating green strips representing the roofs of buildings running north–south. These played a symbolic role, arguing for a more organic, softer approach to urban living than has been common before.

Our view was that environmental considerations should inform the urban morphology (structure, grain, landscape, density, height, massing and so forth) but not dominate it. One needs to understand and use the potential of a site without undermining its sense of place.

Courtyard strips running east–west and strips running north–south were compared. Although detailed calculations were not carried out we believed that as long as the key criteria of being able to use the roofs for photovoltaics (PVs) and active solar collection, and spacing the buildings for ample daylight were met, all of these forms were potentially suitable.

This approach argues for putting taller buildings to the north and avoiding overshadowing. By this stage the site was being seen as a tapestry of warp and weft with additional tension added by interrupting the pattern to create discordant notes. The strands of the tapestry included buildings, water flowing across the site, planting, pedestrian paths and bicycle routes.

We decided that more attention to the environment fortunately did not force an aesthetic upon designers. However, it could inform an aesthetic in which nature and the forces of the sun, wind and water influenced the design in a subtle, sophisticated way and enriched urban living.

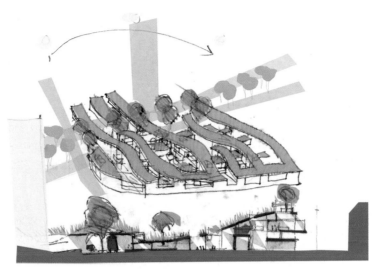

Angel Fields concept sketch

Angel Fields developed scheme

Infrastructure and energy

Ways of producing and delivering energy, dealing with the material flows of water and waste and handling information are evolving very rapidly. To be sustainable our infrastructure of services, plant rooms, pipes and cables will have to be adaptable and flexible to allow for technical and social obsolescence.

The following principles illustrate an approach to energy supply:

- Energy supply for a site in an urban situation should strike the right balance between supply on-site and supply from the region.

- A generic strategy can be developed which incorporates solar energy (passive solar gain, day lighting, active solar collection and PVs), wind energy and energy from waste.

- One way of generating energy from waste is with an on-site digester which produces methane gas from human, kitchen and garden waste. Collection of organic wastes from surrounding neighbourhoods can provide additional feed for the digester.

  This on-site use of waste is an example of changing what is for most of us a linear process into a more efficient and more ecological circular one. It is much closer to both pre-historical and historical precedent. In the Orkney buildings which are the oldest still-standing houses in Europe, kitchen waste played a significant part in the manure used in farming as long as 5000 years ago (Garnham, 2004).

- Residual energy demand can be met from off-site renewable sources such as off-shore wind turbines.

- Flexibility is important. At any given time a flexible strategy allows for a mixture of sources, and over time it permits the introduction of new technologies. These could include, for example, fuel cells, which use hydrogen, as they become more cost-effective.

- The key is a site-wide easily accessible infrastructure and allocation of ample plant-room and distribution space.

In the proposal for a sustainable urban community in Angel Fields, Manchester mentioned previously the urban form and energy strategy were developed together. The energy strategy proposed reduced energy use and the generation of two-thirds of its total estimated energy requirement. The strategy for this proposal is illustrated in the following figure and shows how a strategy can make use of many different and complementary energy sources.

Building design

Very roughly in an urban community, one-third of the energy consumed is associated with buildings, one-third with transport and one-third with food. Reduction of transport energy can be achieved in part through grouping living and working places and encouraging walking, cycling and public transport. Food energy is complex; that is, growing some food on site is a symbolic but important first step. Building energy use and production are the areas where designers can have the most impact.

Building design and urban design are inseparable. At every level from the social to the environmental the two are intertwined. The best spaces and buildings are designed from the 'outside' in and the 'inside' out simultaneously. Their designers imagine what the conditions will be for occupants and passers-by and the results are exciting, rewarding experiences.

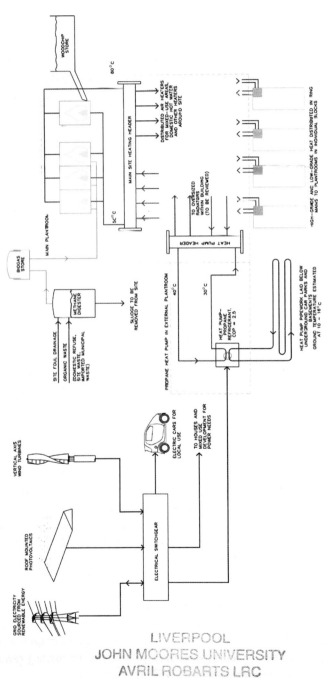

Proposed energy strategy for Angel Fields, Manchester

19

The two principal reasons why your present home is likely to be unsustainable are that it uses too much of everything and everything it does use is supplied in a way that simply cannot go on.

Below are a few key aspects of housing design, which address how we might change this.

Reduce demand: often the most cost-effective first step

- Reduce the demand for energy – both thermal energy for space and water heating, and electrical energy for power and lighting. This is quite possibly the most important step that designers can make towards sustainability.

- Lower the space heating demand by using orientation, form and fenestration to make the most use of passive solar gain.

- Reduce the energy required by having a well-insulated building envelope with high-performance glazing.

- Seal the building tightly and ensure that it is pressure tested so that the air enters by a defined path. This will reduce ventilation heat loss. Fresh air should be of a high quality.

- Use less water, both hot and cold. Energy for domestic hot water can be reduced through judicious water use.

- Integrate the structure and services so that energy use is minimised, summertime overheating is avoided, and the need for artificial cooling becomes insignificant. Include thermal mass in order to even out both internal and external heat gains and to take advantage of night cooling. Control of solar gain, ventilation and thermal mass will all need to work together.

- Further cooling would not normally be needed in well-designed housing but in mixed use developments there could be a small demand. If it is required investigate ambient energy possibilities such as borehole cooling systems.

- Daylighting can significantly reduce the demand for electrical energy.

- The embodied energy in materials should be reduced and waste on site should be minimised.

- The services with their controls should be energy-efficient and 'intelligent'. Occupants should have some control over their environment.

Provide energy in sustainable ways

From Barcelona to Malmo and from Los Angeles to London, cities are waking up to the potential for maximising the opportunities for capturing and producing energy with their buildings. This includes wind energy and energy from the waste produced on site (both human waste and domestic waste) but is principally directed towards the use of solar energy. Using solar potential has four main aspects.

Daylighting

Daylighting and attractive views enhance our experience of our surroundings. In much of Europe, daylight needs to be better treated as the precious commodity that it is.

A varied, poetic mixture of daylight and artificial lighting is desirable. Striking the right balance has significant advantages including reduced CO_2 emissions from power stations. The ongoing improvement of glazing has also meant that it has been possible to provide more natural light with lower heat loss in winter.

Successful spaces are those with good daylight: daylight from two sides, or a wall and roof, can be magical. The 18th century Georgian home with its elegant proportions and tall windows facilitated gracious spaces. It served as a model for the London homes (built in the 1840s, as shown in the illustration) and is also of relevance to us today. Note too that these windows normally had wooden internal shutters, which were used at night to insulate, to maintain comfort and to provide privacy.

In the Parkmount Housing scheme in Belfast by Richard Partington Architects, more than 80% of the apartments have good orientation for sunlight and many have dual aspect living rooms.

1840 London home

21

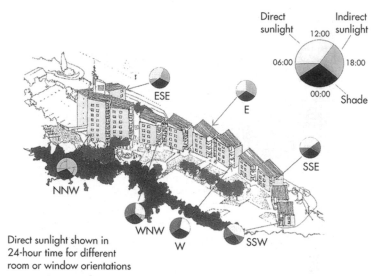

Direct sunlight shown in
24-hour time for different
room or window orientations

Parkmount Housing daylighting analysis

Parkmount completed scheme, Belfast

Passive solar gain

Passive solar gain takes advantage of the solar radiation falling on roofs, walls and, particularly, windows. Letting in the sun during the heating season will help to reduce the demand for fuel. Conversely, in the summer the potential solar gain that could lead to overheating needs to be controlled at the façade.

Palm Housing façade, Coin Street, London

What percentage of a façade should be glazed? There is no easy answer to this (architects will be glad to hear). It will depend on the design intention, orientation, the views out, the layout of the building and the internal spaces, the proportions of the interior spaces, the thermal performance of the window and the wall, to name just a few considerations.

Active solar panels

These actively collect solar energy and transfer it to a fluid, usually water, which is often then used directly or indirectly for domestic hot water.

PVs

These devices convert solar energy directly into electricity, permitting homes to become mini-power stations. They are normally sited on south-facing roofs but can also be placed on south-facing walls.

The Parkmount scheme mentioned previously, is a prime example of a 'solar sculpting' strategy where ambient energy played an important role in determining building form.

23

PVs at Parkmount, Belfast

PVs at The Prior's Estate, Kings Cross, London

All of the roofs were well orientated and sloped for PVs. The illustration shows the photovoltaic panels on one of the roofs. It is intended to install the panels on the other roofs over the next few years. PVs have also been used successfully at the Priors Estate in Kings Cross, London.

Adaptability and evolution

An evolutionary approach of 'design, manage and adapt' is best suited to our future which is uncertain with regard to energy, climate change, social trends and legislation. Getting the basics right and allowing the building to develop is essential.

Both cost and technical constraints require us to consider projects over time. We need to anticipate upgrades and make them as simple as possible (e.g. as simple as insulating the loft of a Victorian terrace house). Another example is that in the latter half of the 19th century in New York building owners often could not afford a lift but they could afford a lift shaft. The lifts were installed after as finances permitted. We need to design our housing in a similar way.

Designs should anticipate continuous evolution. All projects start off with insufficient funding to do what the clients and design teams would like to achieve environmentally. So it is essential to create and draw a development strategy which shows how over time homes and spaces can become more sustainable by, for example, increasing insulation and enlarging the on-site contribution from solar and wind energy.

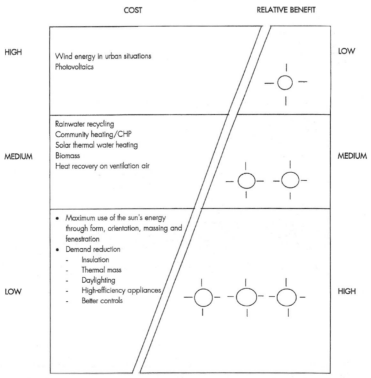

Value for money

Fortunately, there are many things we can do as designers to ensure the sustainability of our projects. We can lay solid foundations for sustainable neighbourhoods even if all the resources are not available at the outset of the project. For example decisions about building form, infrastructure, orientation and daylight strategy are all fundamental for an environmentally sustainable development. Ensuring that opportunities exist for developments to become more sustainable in the future is important. The illustration broadly shows the cost–benefit relationship for a number of initiatives. A note of caution, though: all projects are site specific, and the science and art consist of knowing what is appropriate in a particular context.

Conclusion

Urban design is at a major turning point. Technical progress in energy supply and concern about climate change are encouraging designers to develop urban spaces and building forms suitable for a solar society. Considerations of water, materials, waste, and nature are becoming more and more important in the design of our cities. It is possible to create cities that work well with their regions and are sustainable environmentally, socially and economically. The first steps towards these cities, of which housing forms such a major part, require considerable encouragement and support from all involved.

In summary, guidelines for a more environmentally sustainable and integrated design approach for housing include:

- Form a holistic view – think about the buildings and the three-dimensional space around them, from the energy potential of the earth to that of the sky.

- Take a balanced and plausible approach.

- Reduce demands.

- Generate energy on site from the sun and the wind and, whenever feasible, from waste.

- Encourage circular processes rather than linear ones.

- Plan for flexibility. Social patterns and technologies will change.

- Provide high-quality green spaces.

- Keep individuals at the centre of the process.

Communicating relevant design issues to users is an important element of a sustainable strategy. Chapter 3 focuses on the role of communication for designers.

3

The community agenda

Patrick Hammill
Director, Levitt Bernstein

The people have failed us.
It is time to elect a new one.
Bertold Brecht

Are there people in your photos?

Buildings, neighbourhoods, and all of the spaces in between, matter to the people who use them as much as they matter to the designers that create them. Recognising the different voices and different views of all involved has to be a key component of developing projects that will prove sustainable, both as communities and as investments.

This chapter considers the role of the people that make housing into homes and spaces into places. The design agenda for housing presented in this book cannot be seen in isolation: along with a design-led approach to housing, it is the relationship between residents and designers, and the appropriate communication of design ideas, that delivers quality neighbourhoods.

The residents want their say, whether as tenants of failed social housing or as owner occupiers who have seen the effects of failed development on their streets. For many residents of our cities, towns and villages there is now a strong and positive need to improve *their* neighbourhood. There is an investment – financial, social and emotional – to protect.

The politicians and the legislators also now recognise that to ensure that public investment is effective we need to consider more than individual buildings. Delivering 'sustainable communities' must consider the quality of the spaces in between, the quality of the neighbourhoods, and particularly consider and involve the people who use them.

Looking beyond the boundaries

With rare exceptions clients work within physical and financial boundaries, and want to deliver projects to defined timescales. They need to work within constraints and parameters that can be managed. For them what happens outside of those project boundaries is less controllable, and can be expensive. Local authorities also work within boundaries – when considering planning issues the existing surrounding area is taken as a given, and the project proposals are to be considered within that context. Finally, consultants are trained to analyse a problem within the client's boundaries, define a brief, and design a physical solution. Each of these players, highly trained and committed, makes their contribution to solving the problem that faces them, in a way that it is hoped creates beautiful individual built solutions.

But for most people who use and move around neighbourhoods and cities, what is seen and used, enjoyed, simply accepted, or actively disliked, are the spaces in between or beyond those boundaries. The quality of the streetscape, the sense of place, or the collective image of a series of individual buildings is what defines our journey through the neighbourhood as a pleasant experience or a bad experience.

These issues of place-making are discussed later in the book. But looking beyond the boundaries set by a client brief or a planning department framework, does not only require a holistic design approach, but also engaging and involving the people who experience these places.

What do we mean by consultation? Whatever you decide to call your process – tenants' events, workshops, enquiry by design or consultation – just be honest. Are you providing information that people can take or leave, or are you asking people to contribute, for their views to be seen to be seriously considered within the decision-making process? The latter process is consultation: this is when it is worthwhile for people to contribute their energy and their time.

What kind of involvement?

Broadly there can be two kinds of community involvement in an urban housing project, requiring quite distinct forms of consultation to respond to what can be very different concerns.

Firstly, there are new developments that adjoin existing settlements and affect them. The adjoining residents may welcome the development but may equally feel threatened by more cars through their streets, or by more children in already overstretched schools. They may question whether the new development will add value to or compromise what they enjoy about their neighbourhood. Increasingly these kinds of residents strive to be involved in the decision-making process of new developments in order to protect and enhance their vision of their area.

Secondly, there are new developments that replace or adapt existing settlements and directly affect and possibly re-house current residents. These residents have to be involved in the process. Decisions are being made about their current homes; their future homes are being designed; they are the clients.

From both types of interest group there is much to learn. From both perspectives the concern is to create sustainable neighbourhoods that are able to continuously adapt to the changing needs and demands of the people who live there.

The designer/user relationship

Good urban design brings together many skills – planners, urban designers, landscape architects and architects. Each specialist will individually, and as a member of a team, strive for a quality of development that will last. Each will have their expertise, their remit and their boundaries, and critically each has an involvement within a defined time frame. They will not be the long-term residents; they are the set designers, but not the actors.

Others, who live and work there, will use the spaces and buildings long after that initial design process, and long after the consultants have moved on. As residents or neighbours they may pass through for 5 min or live there for 20 years.

The task for the team leader is to ensure that the role of the 'client user' is recognised, and that the perspective of the 'client user' makes a contribution to the design development. Effective consultation allows designers and policy-makers to work with those most affected, and those who live in or use the area will have particular knowledge and priorities to contribute to the debate. When the views of the residents conflict with those of developers, local authority officers and politicians, the designer has to also learn to be a mediator.

Residents and users may not have the same priorities or use the same language as urban designers, but they do share many of the same values. Residents and people who use a neighbourhood will use expressions such as 'does not feel safe', 'scruffy', 'welcoming', 'nice place to sit', 'somewhere for the kids to grow up' and 'nice place to walk through'. Whilst expressed informally these comments are nonetheless qualitative judgements arising from each individual's understanding and sense of the spaces that they move through.

An important function of consultation is to bring a dialogue that mediates between the concerns of residents faced with change either to their own homes or to their neighbourhood and the bright new world conceived by developers and their consultants. If residents and users understand the logic that drives the proposals the debate will be better informed and able to test solutions to satisfy the concerns of each side. There are no guarantees of agreement but there may be sufficient moderation of the views of each side to at least avoid polarisation, and for users to say 'someone listened and helped create a development that we like'.

Equal access

Designers need to recognise that interested but lay contributors do not speak the consultants' language, probably do not understand drawings no matter how smart the graphics, and have no experience of designers' terms of reference. To communicate there has to be a dialogue using a common ground. The approach needs to be consistent, and to recognise the value of all contributors' views. Consultation is not about patronising people or steering towards a predetermined solution, it is about understanding and recognising each others roles.

The key initiatives for the consultant are given below:

- Avoid all jargon and use honest and plain language.

- Do not de-personalise people's homes by calling them 'units', for example.

- Provide training to enable residents to understand the background policies, project brief and drawings.

- Use models and illustrative views where possible, they are usually more effective than architectural drawings.

- Encourage responses by drawing out issues and asking questions, but allow people to understand in their own time.

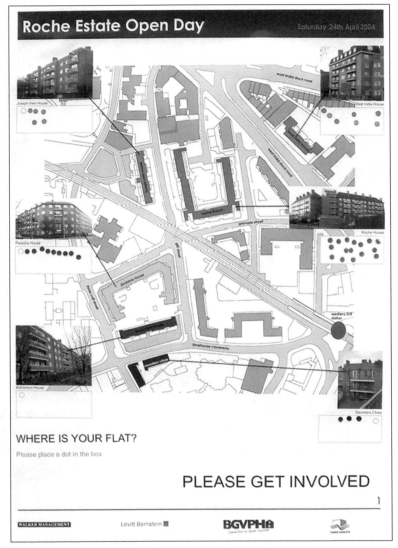

Providing reference points

- Ensure that drawings provide effective reference points so that people can understand the drawings and orientate themselves (the local shop, street names, landmark features, etc.).

- Recognise that effective consultation is based on trust which has to be built over time.

Working with models

Encouraging interaction

Holly Street: engaging for the long term

The regeneration of Holly Street estate in Hackney, London is a good example of how to engage residents in the design process and the benefits that can be gained. Levitt Bernstein, housing architects and master-planners with a long-standing interest in social housing, began work there in 1992.

From 1870 to 1970 Holly Street was a series of streets of mainly Victorian housing, unimproved, and often rented out and multi-occupied. To the east, to the south and to the west were similar areas of housing that were to remain and would be gentrified over the coming years. The new development in 1970 was seen as a bright new beginning, a new urban design, new forms of housing and new standards that owed no allegiance to the past. Those who moved in to the new housing were overjoyed. At last they had their own flat and their own facilities. They could furnish their own home and bring up their family.

Within 10 years the estate was failing. A combination of design and people problems had led to management failure and new tenants did not wish to move there. The current residents were asking the local authority for help and extra resources to halt the decline and improve living conditions. By 1990 many residents felt the estate was simply beyond repair. They wanted to be re-housed elsewhere and for the old housing to be demolished. They had little confidence that any new housing would ever be built. A key role for consultation was to be to convince residents that there was a future for the area.

Developing consultation structures

As is often the case, there was a strong sense of community as many people had lived on the estate for 20 years. If they could get the homes that they wanted in a neighbourhood that met their needs *then* they would like to continue to live there.

To ensure the continuous participation of the residents throughout the design process, a clear consultation structure was put in place. All design decisions were to be taken through an Estate Development Committee comprising elected tenants provided with independent advice. Informing that group were a series of specialist groups, each taking responsibility for particular issues such as the elderly, the under 5s, or housing standards. The potential contribution of residents was not uniform and could best be encouraged by recognising that some residents had very specific interests. Providing for a series of interest groups was a deliberate step.

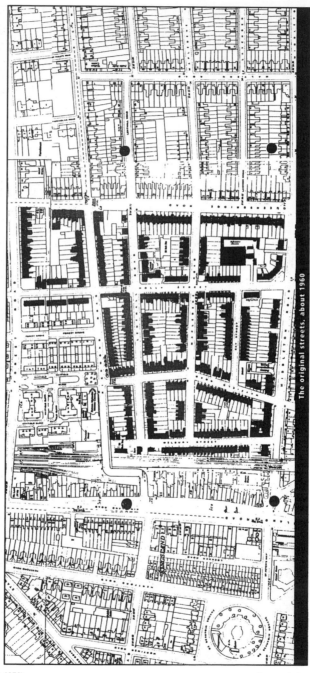

The original streets, about 1960

Holly Street (1870–1970)

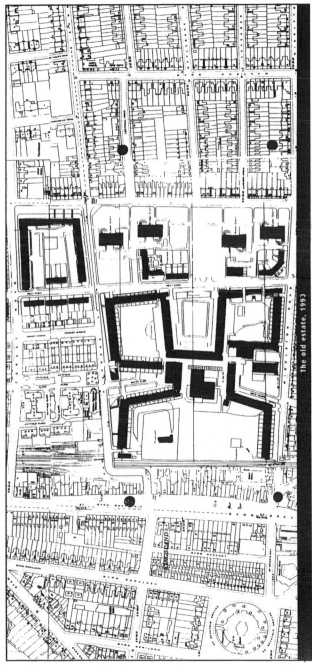

Holly Street (1970) – the new development

Initially there were large public meetings, starting from the basis that all residents had a right to know what was happening, and a questionnaire door-by-door for the whole estate. From that exercise and the Council's earlier work interested residents came forward.

Developing the brief together

The residents' brief was simple: 'give us back the streets that were here before', and 'we do not want to be experimented on again'. The dialogue that followed was to expand and develop shared aims for residents, client and consultants. Over time views and aims became clear. Buildings were to have a hierarchy of urban importance. Homes should be relatively anonymous, ideally simply a door on a street, just like the Victorian streets across the road. For a Holly Street resident that anonymity gained them a place in society. Housing standards were to be the best that could be afforded within the public funding framework. The new square should have the qualities of a true urban square; similar to the historic London squares elsewhere in the borough. Public buildings, the under 5s' centre, the sports and community buildings were to be the buildings representing civic pride. The one remaining tower block, in a prominent position, was to represent the future. No longer was this to be an estate. The new masterplan was to have a network of streets that re-integrated the development area into the surrounding neighbourhood. Public space was to be of high quality, easy to maintain and with streets that were safe to use. All this was to create a sense of place where as a resident you could invite visitors and know that they could find their way to your front door safely.

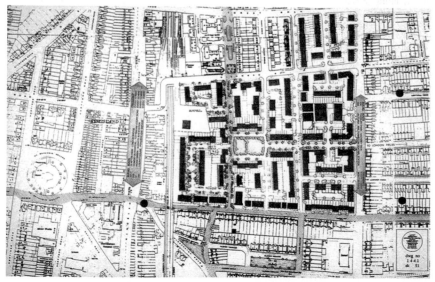

Holly Street, 2002 – the current masterplan

The consultation process enabled residents to re-establish their role as clients, and to have the confidence that the past failures would not be repeated. When it was not possible for residents to achieve all their aspirations they knew why as the process had allowed for a sharing of information that facilitated open and transparent decision-making.

Summary

- Consultation is no longer optional – it is absolutely necessary if a proposed scheme has a significant impact on an existing community.

- Increasingly residents believe that they have a right to contribute to planned changes for their neighbourhood.

- Development of successful and sustainable communities must recognise that the views of those who will live in or will use those spaces and routes are part of the design dialogue.

- People will be pragmatic and do know that difficult choices have to be made in any development project, but they would rather be a part of the decision-making process than have a third-party to make the choices.

- Those who wish to contribute will not share professionals' language nor choose to understand it. Common languages based on common sense are required.

- Training should be provided to help the understanding of plans and models as well as the terms of reference that constrain final decisions.

- Simply recognise that effective dialogue is based on trust, shared language and common goals.

- Be brave, if that dialogue happens then each in their own language will find common urban design objectives.

- Poor design leads to alienation between people and place. Engaging residents and users helps to identify and address the important design issues.

Chapter 4 looks at some of the social needs and aspirations for housing that are commonly recognised by designers and users alike.

4

The social agenda

Housing is different wherever we go, and so should it be. But what every housing scheme has in common is an attempt, through the design process, to create an environment that responds to social needs and aspirations.

Good housing projects, whilst all different, ultimately constitute good living environments. They do so to different extents, for different reasons, using different design approaches, as will be seen in the case studies later on, in this book. And they do so because designers and users alike, consciously or not, have commonly-held values. This is what place-making is about – designers concerning themselves with social issues.

Social places

Fundamental to understanding design issues for housing is the idea that the physical form of the urban environment is a central aspect of the social world itself. Spatial solutions affect social action by setting constraints, providing opportunities and fostering activities. Social values and processes, and the physical form of housing projects are therefore mutually inclusive dimensions of housing provision and must be considered as part of the same process. It is these concerns about commonly held values, like sustainability, community and safety, that make designers think about the relationships between buildings and spaces, not only the buildings and spaces themselves.

These social values, however, often become words that are bandied about, inserted into design statements to get the ticks against the right boxes. But this does not devalue their importance. Most designers will want to make their buildings more than objects in space, or spaces without context, and in order to do so they have to design within a frame of reference of social values. These social values, and the socio-spatial qualities that realise them, are discussed in this chapter.

Social values

What are the values that are important to society? That of course depends on which society or culture we are talking about, and the values that are discussed here are in no way a definitive list of concerns. A good place to start, however, for any society, is to look at sustainability and its themes: sustainability is, after all, about making good places that last.

Sustainability is an overriding social value, influenced and complemented in turn by the provision of choice, safety and a sense of community or neighbourliness. Thus, if a place enables these values to be realised, then people will want to live there, and the place will be sustained. None of these values or qualities is exclusive, indeed they all influence or contain elements of each other.

Choice

Choice is about a lack of restriction, not compromising future options, a more democratic way of using the built environment. We all like to have a choice of how to get somewhere – to walk, cycle, take a bus, or even take a different route. And we all like to know that we are not 'stuck' somewhere and that our life choices will broaden rather than be restricted.

In order to work towards a system for built form that encompasses the fundamental value of choice, it must be noted that the same built form can have radically different implications for different people depending on their respective resources. Essentially, there is a direct relationship between places and the resources available to the people who use them.

Current culture allows people with economic power to make more choices than poor people about where and how they live, work, play, and travel. It is in the physical realm of the city that this social and economic inequality can start to be addressed – in the configuration of urban spaces and places. The most positive ones are those that offer the most choice or restrict reliance on further resources. The most negative are those that discourage choice through lavish use of external resources, such as the car.

But no one designs in an ideal world, and each project has its own clientele and context. As will be seen in the next section of the book, some housing projects restrict opportunities for choice more than others. For example, the schemes that are closer to public transport require less parking and are therefore available to a greater range of people. Where there is little or no public transport, and a higher requirement for parking, the challenge becomes how to incorporate the parking sensitively, without compromising other social needs.

In terms of the built environment, which lasts a long time, particularly at the level of street systems and buildings, choice is maintained by ensuring that future possibilities are not compromised by present day developments. In this respect, the concerns of sustainability are a central theme.

The concerns of sustainability are also closely related to the provision of choice at a broader level of planning. Planning for mixed communities allows people of varying economic power to choose between a variety of different buildings, locations, and neighbourhoods in which to live. These choices are supported by the provision of quality public transport and the integration of neighbourhood services, and facilities that meet a range of needs.

'Community' and 'neighbourliness'

The frequently debated concept of 'community' is commonly open to two very different interpretations. The first interpretation of community involves the idea of physical environments where 'community' can be 'built'. The second, and more appropriate interpretation of the term 'community', involves interest groups with a common purpose.

In this time of increasing fragmentation, unpredictability, changing demographics and social trends, it is important to ask whether the creation of well-designed 'built' communities is an appropriate way of dealing with our current urban condition. As much as it can be a basis for social inclusion, designed community can also be the basis for xenophobic and, at times, divisive social and political practices.

It is clear that in today's world, community is neither easily designed, nor necessarily place-based, but built rather by the actions of people over time. What inspires people to join together seems to be mutual interest rather than geographic location. In addition, phones, cars, and air travel have long made it possible to establish and sustain important social relationships outside of one's physical neighbourhood, and often communities are created by people who live in different neighbourhoods, even cities.

This idea of community evolves further when taking into account the widespread use of the Internet. For some, virtual communities are places where conviviality is found and where community is built and sustained. It is now possible even to have supportive and intimate relationships between people who never see, smell, touch, or hear each other.

Given this view of the world, it follows that the problems of housing cannot be solved through the 'creation' of physical communities alone. Communities cannot be built. People create communities, and these communities grow and change all the time. Places, however, can be built. And, it is the role of designers to make sure that these places are not designed for single communities but encourage neighbourliness. This is because neighbourliness is sustainable: it does not rely on knowing names or belonging to a committee, but promotes a safe environment. In the design of physical housing environments, it is the task of urban designers to address the current social context of a 'society of strangers' (Sennett, 1993). In actual physical design terms this means that relationships between users and strangers should be encouraged.

The urban street as described by Jane Jacobs shows how the ideal neighbourly community works in contrast to the physically bound idea of 'community', and it reflects upon the effectiveness of open or structured space to further the opportunities for users. The urban scenario embraces the stranger as someone who enriches rather than threatens the local environment. The people who live here do not know all each other but there is a built-in surveillance system that ensures safety. This is signified in the story she tells about a young girl struggling with a man on the street (Jacobs, 1961: 48). This 'do-it-yourself' surveillance is what has been described above as 'neighbourliness'. Though this approach may not be enough in places where security is a big issue, it demonstrates a solution for a safe environment, which does not have to resort to the extreme of the introverted communities, and the negative implications they have for other people.

In essence, places are well-loved when people feel safe in them. But this does not come down to a sense of 'community', as it is not necessary to know everyone's name to feel safe. It comes down to the kind of PLACE it is, and the extent to which the place encourages neighbourliness and support. This is not to say that issues of community are not important. They are, especially in terms of the participation and enablement of user groups in the housing design process, as we saw in Chapter 3. But they have to go hand in hand with the establishment of management and maintenance systems that ensure the longevity and success of the project.

Safety

Safety and security are significant issues at a variety of levels – in the home, in the immediate space around the home, on the routes to and from work or local facilities, and in the streets and spaces of the wider neighbourhood. Safety needs to be in place at all levels, and not just through the means of security alarms and CCTV cameras. Safety has to be a factor of what kind of place it is – from homes to streets to neighbourhoods. Then, and only then, will safety be both effective and sustainable.

The social issue of safety is one that predominates over others in many social contexts. Fears that lead to an emphasis on design for safety are entirely reasonable and justified but have led to an unfortunate attachment to suburban models and their perceived norms for a safe environment, such as cul-de-sacs, enclaves, and defensive developments.

These suburban models have nothing in common with the varied, lively and permeable urban quarters of compact cities, where safety is more a result of neighbourliness and mutual support. In fact, suburban models encourage a greater reliance on passive surveillance by residents rather than active surveillance by people, users and strangers, moving through the residential neighbourhood. Also, while a cul-de-sac, enclave or defensive development can offer a level of safety to its immediate users, it has a negative impact on other areas that surround it, which suffer from reduced surveillance, resulting in variable public safety in the overall urban environment.

Urban places encourage interactions in the public realm through increased pedestrian activity and vitality, and whilst this paradigm absorbs the presence of strangers as necessary elements of a natural policing system, it also relies on positive distinctions between public and private space. This is an important design issue, which is discussed later.

On looking at safety, consideration should not just be given to the principles of connectivity and vitality on a local scale, but also to the principle of uniform safety in the overall urban context. A street equipped to handle strangers relies on the vitality and interaction that results from connected street networks at both a local and global level.

Socio-spatial qualities

Social values are realised through a series of socio-spatial qualities. They do this by describing how a spatial quality can confer a social quality. The socio-spatial qualities of permeability, legibility, adaptability or flexibility, energy efficiency, variety, activity or vitality, and privacy discussed here are not an exhaustive list: there may be other qualities that are more valued in particular societies. They are also by no means mutually exclusive; in fact they are interwoven with a complexity that reflects the subtle relationships between social issues and physical urban form.

The provision of choice in urban environments encourages mobility for all users of public space networks by offering improved accessibility of places through a variety of routes. This applies at the level of streets as well as linkages within blocks, buildings and individual units. Improved accessibility, or **permeability**, not only improves choice but it also contributes to neighbourliness and safety, by increasing the numbers of people on the streets and thereby chances of contact and built-in surveillance. This quality of permeability is also highly sustainable in its allowance for future responses at an urban scale. An open public space network can easily accommodate a change of use.

For example, car use can be changed to pedestrian use with the small intervention of bollards in a street.

In order to effectively access the choices provided, it is necessary for places to be understood and easily found, through both physical form and activity patterns. This quality of **legibility** is important in housing developments and is best promoted by layouts that are on a grid or which lead to a central focus, the use of physical landmarks, small blocks and the vitality generated by active frontages, and varieties of uses. As important, legibility also contributes to safety and neighbourliness in the public realm by ensuring that routes are clear and understandable.

The kinds of buildings and spaces required to support sustainable environments need to absorb and accommodate differences, appeal to the widest number of users, and have the potential to accept a continuously changing and unpredictable range of activities. The quality required to do this is **adaptability or flexibility**, and it contributes to the sustainability of developments; to the provision of choice, as users' needs and aspirations change over time; and to neighbourliness and safety, which both rely on activity and vitality, and which are easier to achieve consistently with a flexible approach to the design of buildings and spaces.

Closely linked to adaptability is the quality of **energy efficiency**. Sustainability not only demands that buildings and spaces should be adaptable enough to change and accommodate different uses over time, but also that energy should not be wasted in tearing down and rebuilding buildings every time needs and aspirations change.

Energy efficiency is not just an important consideration at this level of sustainability. It is also vital at a building level and a global urban level. At a building level, an important factor contributing to energy efficiency is the need to maximise the use of ambient energy through design, rather than importing electric light, temperature control and mechanical ventilation. In this way, building depth, height, access, and response to aspect are all important design considerations. (These issues were discussed in more detail in Chapter 2.) This applies not only to the design of buildings and spaces themselves but also to the effect that those buildings may have on adjoining spaces and buildings. At a global urban level energy efficiency is the foundation of the compact city paradigm, with its emphasis on urban concentration and reduction in automobile dependence and increased pedestrian activity.

Promoting a **variety** of uses increases choices of experiences for users, and is sustainable in terms of dealing with dynamic social environments. Successful urban settings usually make a variety of resources available with mixed-use developments. While it is not always possible to encourage mixed-use in housing developments, variety can be achieved through the design of robust buildings that can accommodate change of use over time, as well as providing a range of choice of dwelling types to cater for a variety of household types.

Closely linked to variety is the quality of **activity or vitality**. Whilst mixed-use develop-ments enhance safety and neighbourliness because of the variety of activities taking place over an extended time period, it is often difficult to achieve a mix of uses in new settlements where there is less demand for shops and facilities. In housing developments, therefore, safety relies primarily on the vitality of the public realm, generated by positive relationships between buildings and spaces, and by the presence of other people who become a source of comfort and safety. Vitality therefore relies on interaction through pedestrian activity, which is encouraged by permeable and legible street networks.

In contrast to vitality is the quality of **privacy**. Promoting surveillance and safety in the street is good, but the need for vitality should not compromise the right of users to privacy within their dwellings and associated spaces. Vitality and privacy, therefore, rely on the distinction between public and private space, and the gradient of activity between them. Privacy is a quality that is, somewhat paradoxically, aligned with the theme of neighbourliness: it respects the needs of the individual, but is balanced with the need for vitality in the public realm.

In summary, a frame of reference for designers could include the following important social **values**:

- Sustainability

- Choice

- Community and neighbourliness

- Safety

Socio-spatial qualities are the designer's tools for realising these values and could include the following:

- Permeability

- Legibility

- Adaptability/flexibility

- Energy efficiency

- Activity/vitality

- Privacy

These values and qualities form the foundation of the design agenda in the second part of this book.

Part Two

5

A DESIGN AGENDA

The 'design agenda' of a project may also be referred to as the 'design rationale'. Whatever it is called, it should describe the design decision (*what* has been done), the social values that it addresses (*why* it has been done) and which socio-spatial qualities are helping to achieve this (*how* it is being done).

The design agenda, or rationale, of a project should address a set of issues, some that are generic to most projects, and some that are specific to the opportunities and constraints of that particular project. Therefore, each project will have its own unique agenda. It is for this reason that the agenda presented in this chapter is not trying to be a comprehensive list of all issues that should ever be explored for housing: as well as exploring a series of important issues, its function is to demonstrate a methodology for the design, or communication, process.

The design process should evolve through various layers of decision-making, from the strategic issues of connected streets and building form, to the more detailed decisions about building/space interfaces. This process is reflected in the agenda of issues that are addressed in a project. The issues should not be seen as either architecture or urban design — the design process for both should be completely integrated. The design agenda illustrated here does not go into architectural detail, at least not the kind of detail that is critical for good place-making. Of course, this approach is not to disregard the importance of detailed architectural design and the need for richness and expression to add colour to our environments. Rather, there is an emphasis on getting the early decisions right, providing a palette or platform for the delights that architectural expression can offer.

Whether it is to analyse a project, to describe it to fellow designers, clients or future users, or to inform the design process itself, the design agenda of a housing project needs to follow a logic. The order or logic should correspond to the various levels of physical urban structure, and the impact of design decisions made at each level. It will therefore start with the most strategic design decisions to be made, and follow with the more detailed or specific decisions. To establish an appropriate sequence for an agenda of issues, concepts of urban morphology are useful to identify the various levels of physical urban form at which our decisions are made.

URBAN MORPHOLOGY

Starting at the most abstract level, the two most basic morphological elements are **public open space** and **private development blocks** or **plots**. **Built form** then mediates between urban public space and urban private space. The **buildings** and **spaces** themselves are less embedded morphological elements but require more detailed consideration, while the **interfaces** and **thresholds** are the most malleable, and where an individual and specific response becomes particularly relevant.

Looking at urban elements in this way allows a distinction to be made between 'framework' elements (streets and blocks) and 'infill' elements (buildings, spaces and interfaces). The framework elements are the ones that need to be done right if a project is to be sustainable: decisions about the form of streets and public spaces and development blocks are far more strategic in terms of their longevity, as they are the least easy to change. For example, a cul-de-sac arrangement does not allow for future changes while an open grid street network offers choices and can manage movement without using built form barriers.

In contrast, the less strategic 'infill' elements like the interfaces between buildings and spaces, private and public, are often a level that shows the most cultural variation. For example, privacy will be more important in some cultural contexts, while in others front spaces may be used as an extension of a living space. Design decisions made at this level are as important as the decisions about streets and blocks as they all contribute to the resident's and street user's experience, but they are less critical in terms of their adaptability as the space is 'softer' and easier to manipulate or change.

Whilst concepts of spatial structure are useful to identify the elements of physical urban form, they are also significant in the important debate about the use of design coding. If coding is prescriptive at the strategic design decision-making levels it will be more effective in the interests of a rich and sustainable urbanism than codes and rules about architectural style, where variety and richness could be compromised. Ultimately, the key is to maintain a balance between prescription and flexibility. This means keeping the rules where they are needed (where they are less easy to reverse), and allowing creative freedom for designers and users where their decisions have less impact on the longevity of the place.

INTRODUCING THE ISSUES

The issues outlined here are independent of style and architectural expression. Whilst there is a need for buildings to fit into or enhance their context, this is done most importantly at an urban level, in the arrangement of buildings and spaces, and the massing and 'grain' of the development more than through architectural treatment. So, though detailed architectural issues do not form a part of this design agenda, they are certainly recognised in the case studies that follow, especially where they are a dominant feature of a scheme.

It is important to note too that none of these issues stand alone – they are all inextricably bound to each other – qualitative and quantitative, strategic and detailed. If one were to draw a matrix of all the relationships, it would be a very dense and complicated one, with degrees of emphasis on certain relationships depending on the context and requirements of the projects themselves. The agenda is also not suggesting a list of issues to be addressed in a linear fashion. The design process should of course be iterative, paying due importance to the most strategic decisions.

Last but not least, design guidance and principles can only go so far. As every designer knows, things really start to sparkle when there is a site. Indeed, the talented designer can often extract a lot more value out of a highly constrained site. And it is only when there is a site that the balancing and compromising come into play – a potential richness through the challenge of the site, waiting to be tapped. This we will see in abundance with the case studies in the next section. In the meantime, let us take a look at a sample list of issues, without the context of a real site, which can be used as a checklist, a method of describing a scheme, or a 'design agenda'.

THE AGENDA

Making connections

- *Homes should be connected to facilities and amenities.*

- *Grids facilitate connections. They do not have to be orthogonal and rigid and can take on many forms and shapes. The key is that grids provide permeable movement networks.*

- *Permeable or connected movement networks (streets, paths and public spaces) provide choices for pedestrian routes. Maximising choice encourages people to walk or cycle.*

- *If public spaces like parks and squares are absorbed into these networks, pedestrian activity is further encouraged. And these spaces become more interesting as places to linger and watch the world go by.*

- *Activity in public routes and spaces makes them safer. These spaces can then become a focus for local residents, adding to the vitality of the public realm.*

Above   *Play area at the confluence of streets, Gracia, Barcelona*
Right   *Connected routes and spaces*
Below   *An outdoor sitting room, Venice*

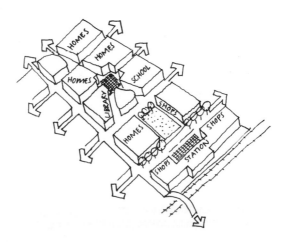

Providing green areas and corridors

- Green areas are important elements in place-making: they enhance the legibility of a place and they increase the variety of uses in a place.

- Green areas and corridors can be for biotic support and public amenity – these can be part of the public or private realm, and some can be specifically for biotic support only.

- These areas need to be as connected as possible to each other – they can even form another network layered over or part of the permeable network for people.

- Designing with landscape concepts from the outset gives schemes a landscape language to tie buildings and spaces together as integral components of the place.

Above Linear park, Bastille Viaduct, Paris
Left Housing and waterways, Greenwich Millennium Village, London
Below Aquapunkt Dam, Bo01, Malmo

Treating the street as a place

- With permeable movement networks and the focus on choice and pedestrian activity, it is important to minimise car dominance and make streets into safe and attractive places to be.

- This can be done by accommodating all users in the realm of the street and treating the street as a positive space.

- The key to a pedestrian friendly neighbourhood is the reduction of vehicle speed and the reclamation of much more of the street area for pedestrians.

- Accommodating parking in the street also keeps eyes on the cars and activity in the street.

- Pedestrian friendly neighbourhoods also rely on the landscape of the streets. The environmental quality of streets needs to be delivered through good landscape design where all elements – paving, lighting, seating, street furniture and signage, trees and planting – are well considered and form a legible street character.

- Finally, just as with any public space, one of the most important ways of making a street into a place is by considering the relationship of the street with the buildings that frame it.

Above   Public art and seating as part of the street, Olympic Village, Barcelona
Right   Pedestrian priority street, Bo01, Malmo
Below   Street for all users, San Sebastian

Laying out the built form

- *Permeable movement networks are not effective and safe unless they are complemented by a building form that defines the routes and spaces.*

- *Aligning buildings along and around public spaces and streets gives them a sense of enclosure, reinforcing their identity and legibility.*

- *By orientating active 'fronts' to streets and public spaces, and inactive 'backs' to the private realm, activity is encouraged in streets and public spaces, and security and privacy is maintained in 'back' spaces or courts.*

- *This way of arranging buildings often generates a perimeter block form, which can take on any shape.*

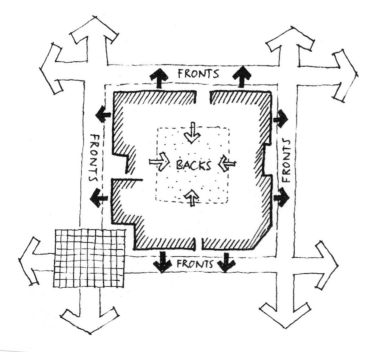

Orienting fronts and backs

Built form defining the street

Absorbing diversity

- The flexibility of the perimeter block form can absorb different residential building types from apartment buildings to terraced houses, as well as other uses.

- Perimeter blocks also facilitate the integration of different housing tenures, without having to create completely separate buildings, which then often have problems with the use and management of the spaces between the buildings. With a terraced or perimeter block form, buildings can still have separate access from the street, each with their own entrance.

- The flexibility of the terrace form and the perimeter block also encourages a variety of architectural treatments and a range of expressions.

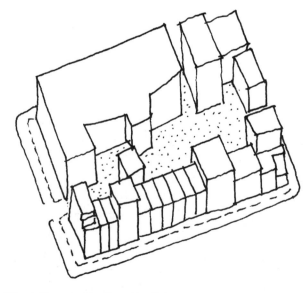

Left   Different building types and forms in a perimeter block
Right   Terrace forms encourage variety of expression, Borneo Island, Amsterdam

Defining public and private space

- *Built form should mediate between public and private space.*

- *This gives residents the opportunity to choose between activity and privacy.*

- *The extent to which buildings make the distinction between public and private space will depend on required levels of security and penetration into the blocks and/or buildings.*

- *The boundaries between public and private space are easy to manage with perimeter blocks, which can have varying levels of enclosure. Some blocks only require the suggestion of enclosure, with gaps between the buildings where access is managed by natural surveillance or gates. In other blocks that require more security and/or privacy, the building form can be a solid and continuous barrier between inside and outside or public and private space.*

Above   Entrances to courts can introduce breaks in the perimeter block form, LIND, San Diego
Right   Perimeter block buildings mediate to different degrees between public and private space
Below   Private courtyards inside the perimeter block, Little Italy Neighbourhood Development (LIND), San Diego

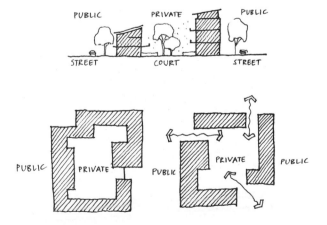

Creating a relationship between buildings and spaces

- *Buildings can affect the quality of public spaces in two ways: the way their uses interface with the space, and how their volume and mass frames or encloses the space. These are all important considerations for the legibility of streets and spaces.*

- *When buildings and spaces are considered together they make a positive contribution to the quality of the public realm.*

- *This successful relationship relies on the firm distinction between 'fronts' and 'backs' of buildings. The front of a building should ideally include its primary entrance or entrances and where this is not the case, the front should most certainly accommodate the primary aspect of the building with as many windows and activity-generating functions as possible.*

- *Building fronts should always face the public realm, whether it is a street, public walkway, park or square.*

- *It is not only the activity generated by the building but also its form that affects the quality of public spaces. Building heights should be proportional to the spaces they align. For example, wider streets need higher buildings to define them. But this has to be balanced against the negative effects of overshadowing.*

Left   Apartments fronting onto the pedestrian promenade, Bo01, Malmo
Above Houses overlooking the street, Kettner Row, San Diego

Arranging the building mass

- *Building massing is often a factor of required densities for housing projects. High density need not be negative, and if the building mass is sensitively and appropriately arranged, the places created can be very positive.*

- *Building mass should be arranged to ensure that streets and public spaces are well defined, legible, and that important amenity spaces are not overshadowed.*

- *The terrace form of development, as opposed to the tower block model, performs a much more positive role in street definition. It can often yield similar densities to towers but with the benefit of private garden provision and more secure amenity space for residents inside the block, and surveillance of the street.*

- *Tower blocks can be very positive in terms of density and landmark status – they also provide good views for residents. However, they also need to make good places at the ground level, just like any other building. And developments with tower blocks have a bigger responsibility to provide quality communal outdoor space.*

PAVILION FORM   TERRACE FORM

Above   Terrace forms define the street
well
Right   Tower design should address
what happens on the ground

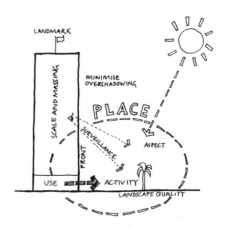

Optimising solar potential and good aspect

- *Sensitive orientation of buildings can make them more energy efficient through passive solar gain, daylight, photovoltaic modules and solar panels.*

- *Overshadowing of public and private amenity spaces should be avoided as this will discourage activity in them. The scale and massing of buildings has a large part to play in this, especially when it comes to positioning taller buildings. Allowing light penetration into blocks through gaps between buildings or variations in building height can also improve the quality of amenity spaces.*

- *Balanced against the need to avoid overshadowing of spaces around and between buildings is the need to provide as many units as possible with good aspect, whether for views or good orientation for sunlight.*

- *Where possible, dwellings should have a choice of aspect, either front and back or on two sides for corner buildings.*

- *Single aspect dwellings should always face either a good view, good sun orientation or, ideally, both.*

- *Single aspect dwellings are often more suitable as wide frontages with shallow floor plans, while dual aspect dwellings are usually suitable with narrow frontages and deep plans.*

- *Single aspect dwellings rely on good solar orientation on their frontage (towards south if in the northern hemisphere), while dual aspect dwellings are more flexible as they provide choice of aspect. Ideally, dual aspect units should lie close to an east–west access so that they can benefit from morning and afternoon sun.*

- *Privacy between units should be addressed by considering aspect across streets and courtyards. This can be managed by planning the arrangement of habitable rooms within the dwellings appropriately, varying the building line to create oblique views, and providing screening and landscaping that does not compromise surveillance.*

Allowing light into the block

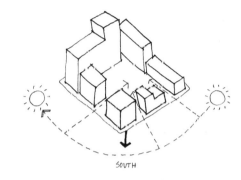

SOUTH

Dwelling plan forms depend on aspect

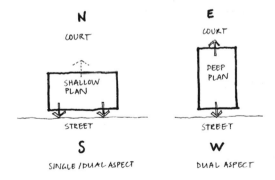

Managing aspect to control privacy

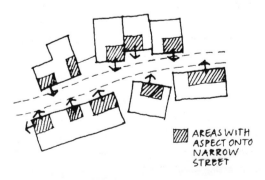

Managing and integrating parking

- Ideally, as much parking should be provided in the street as possible, without dominating the street with cars or compromising pedestrian safety. This relies on good layout and street landscaping, but is very effective in keeping activity in the street.

- Even if parking is not provided on the street, primary entrances to buildings should still be off the street, with additional secondary access from private parking areas provided if necessary.

- Where parking is provided in courts or squares inside the block, it should be designed as a legible element of the overall landscape strategy, preferably as a shared surface space seamlessly connected to building entrances and other public amenities. Smaller pockets of parking (no more than 10–15 spaces) are more easily absorbed into an attractive outdoor space than large, dominating areas of parking. It is also important that the parking areas are well overlooked and that clear and safe pedestrian routes between parking areas and the entrances to homes are provided.

- Decking over parking between buildings inside a block can be a very positive move – parking requirements are met, the cars do not dominate, and an amenity space for residents can be created on the deck. The success of this will rely on the design of the parking, ensuring good lighting, security and access to dwellings. It is also important to maintain activity on the ground floor of the building especially where it interfaces with the public realm. This activity can be generated by single aspect dwellings where appropriate, community facilities, or commercial properties.

- Basement parking, although expensive, clears the space between buildings for residents' amenity. Again good lighting, security and access are important. Basement parking often necessitates the ground floor of buildings to be raised so that the basement can be ventilated. This can be beneficial for the privacy of ground floor dwellings but can also create

Left Top   Communal gardens inside
              the block, above parking,
              Greenwich Millennium
              Village, London
Left Bottom   Integral garage does not
              dominate the façade,
              Kettner Row, San Diego
Right Top   Parking in courts should
              be well landscaped and
              overlooked by
              surrounding buildings
Right Bottom Deck over parking with
              apertures for light and
              trees, Nieuw Terbrugge,
              Rotterdam (Mecanoo)

bland facades if raised too high. Disabled access also needs to be considered if the ground floor dwellings are not level with the street.

- Garages that are designed as an integral part of houses can be very popular, but have to be carefully designed so that they do not dominate the facades of the houses. This is a detailed design consideration and can be achieved in a number of ways, for example by lowering the level of the garage and/or giving the garage as small an entrance as possible.

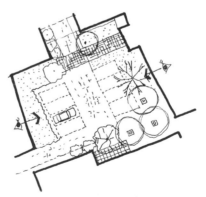

Providing frequent and convenient access

- *Entrances to buildings should be from the street (public realm) and as frequent as possible. This is helped when buildings are narrower and closer together in a terrace form.*

- *With apartment buildings, regular points of access to buildings mean that fewer units share lobbies, giving an opportunity for increased 'ownership' of common areas, and more privacy for residents.*

- *Allowing access to run through from the street to the private space or courtyard at the rear of the building allows easy access from the units above into the shared space and amenities, and articulates the choices between activity and privacy.*

- *Addressing the needs of all when considering access, especially the disabled and elderly, allows the flexible use of buildings despite occupier profiles changing with time.*

Right Above   Apartment buildings
                should have frequent
                entrances off the street
Right Below   Terrace Housing, Bo01,
                Malmo
Below   Terrace Housing,
                Greenwich Millennium
                Village, London

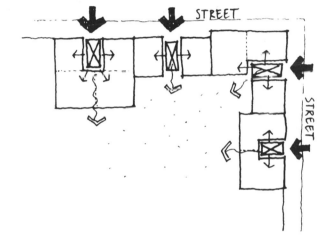

Mixing uses/recycling/building in flexibility

- *Achieving a mix of uses is a key dimension of sustainable high density urban housing, providing facilities and amenities for residents and a varied and active public neighbourhood.*

- *Where possible residential schemes should either incorporate other uses, or be designed to accommodate them in the future. This is energy efficient in terms of reducing the need to pull down and rebuild buildings as their uses change over time.*

- *Recycling and adapting existing buildings for housing is preferable to new-build where feasible. Large industrial spaces to be adapted to housing often offer opportunities for exciting mixes of dwellings and uses.*

- *Where a mix of uses is not feasible at the time of development, future active uses should be encouraged with the design of flexible spaces on at least the ground floor level of residential buildings. This entails ensuring that access from the street is as direct as possible, and that the potential use will not interfere with residential uses adjacent or above.*

- *Integrated garages can be very useful for building in flexibility as they can be converted into workspaces that are directly accessible from the street.*

- *Houses and apartments should be designed for future adaptability, offering occupiers the opportunity to modify and personalise their homes as the family structure changes, or when they want to accommodate workspaces or other activities.*

- *Homes can be designed to be extendable from the sides or backs or up into the roof. Internal layouts can be changed if structures have large spans and internal walls are not load bearing. Adaptability is a detailed design consideration and an opportunity for innovation.*

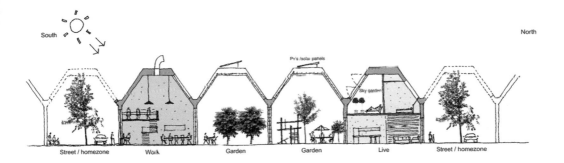

South   North

Pv's /solar panels

Sky garden

Street / homezone   Work   Garden   Garden   Live   Street / homezone

Above   *Proposal for conversion of*
                factory space into live/work
                spaces, Darlington, UK
Left Below   *Garage converted into*
                workspace, Kettner Row,
                San Diego
Right Below   *Ground floor dwellings can*
                be adaptable for other
                uses in the future

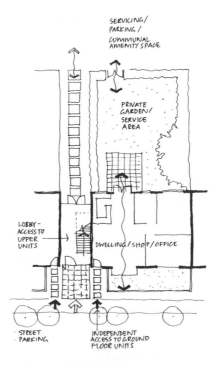

SERVICING/
PARKING /
COMMUNAL
AMENITY SPACE

PRIVATE
GARDEN/
SERVICE
AREA

LOBBY –
ACCESS TO
UPPER
UNITS

DWELLING / SHOP/OFFICE

STREET
PARKING

INDEPENDENT
ACCESS TO GROUND
FLOOR UNITS

Providing spaces around the home

- *Spaces around the home form important interfaces between inside and outside, private and public space.*

- *These interface spaces can also be used as privacy screens.*

- *In many cases these private and semi-private spaces become an extension of the home, giving residents further choice on how and where to spend their time.*

- *A range of private and semi-private outdoor spaces gives residents a choice of spaces, which may be more sunny, more private, or provide better views.*

- *Back gardens or patios should be designed to maintain privacy but encourage surveillance. Where private gardens abut semi-private communal spaces like play areas, raising the private garden level helps to define the garden as well as to facilitate overlooking of the communal space.*

Right Above   Communal decked amenity space extending from the home, Nieuw Terbrugge, Rotterdam (Mecanoo)
Right Middle   Communal amenity space inside the block, Hulme, Manchester
Right Below   Balconies and terraces add interest to the building form, Bo01, Malmo
Below   Private gardens inside the block – managing privacy and surveillance

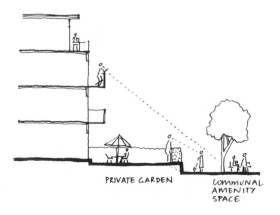

PRIVATE GARDEN

COMMUNAL AMENITY SPACE

Meeting the ground – thresholds and interfaces

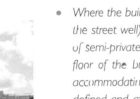

- Interfaces between the buildings and spaces control the privacy of homes and safety in the spaces they adjoin.

- Where the buildings are high enough (and they perform the role of defining the street well) buildings can be set back from the street to create a zone of semi-private space that protects the privacy of the home on the ground floor of the building. This front interface space can be very effective for accommodating refuse and recycling bins. When these areas are well defined and attractive they also serve to protect the privacy of the home further.

- Where buildings are only two or three stories high (usually houses) and the streets are not of the narrow mews type, other mechanisms must be used to protect privacy, while enhancing surveillance of the street. Level changes are very effective for this purpose but then create a new problem of access for the disabled and elderly. This problem can be overcome with a number of designed solutions (see Palm Housing, Coin Street).

- Whatever design solution is used at these sensitive thresholds, it must strike a balance between creating privacy for residents and safety for passers by on the street. Safety relies on natural surveillance from buildings, and activity emanating from them. Different cultures, each with their own priorities for privacy, will deal with these interfaces in different ways.

Above Water channels and planting give terrace houses a semi-private zone on a narrow street, Bo01, Malmo

Right Level changes and setbacks help privacy, but street enclosure must be maintained

Below Small, screened front terraces protect the privacy of ground floor homes, Greenwich Millennium Village, London

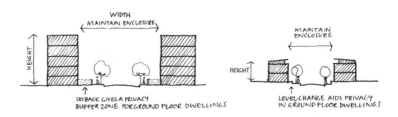

SETBACK GIVES A PRIVACY BUFFER ZONE FOR GROUND FLOOR DWELLINGS

LEVEL CHANGE AIDS PRIVACY IN GROUND FLOOR DWELLINGS

In summary, this design agenda for urban housing has included the following design issues for consideration:

Making connections	Choice, permeability, activity, safety
Providing green areas and corridors	Legibility, variety, activity
Treating the street as a place	Safety, activity
Layout out the built form	Legibility, activity, neighbourliness, safety
Absorbing diversity	Flexibility, variety
Defining public and private space	Choice, safety, activity, privacy
Creating a relationship between buildings and spaces	Safety, activity, legibility
Arranging the building mass	Safety, legibility, energy efficiency
Optimising solar potential and good aspect	Choice, energy efficiency, privacy
Managing and integrating parking	Safety, legibility, flexibility
Providing frequent and convenient access	Activity, privacy, flexibility
Mixing uses/building in flexibility	Variety, activity, adaptability, energy efficiency
Providing spaces around the home	Choice, safety, privacy
Meeting the ground – thresholds and interfaces	Safety, privacy, activity

This is not an exhaustive list, and demonstrates an approach to the sequence with which our design issues should be considered. The case studies that follow will illustrate how these design issues can be addressed, as well as bring to light their own specific design issues that are particular to their context and development requirements.

6

Introduction to the case studies

An agenda of design issues has been presented. The following chapters look at a sample of projects, or case studies, which reveal the complexity of these design issues and how responses to each design challenge can vary. In some cases the 'rules' will seem to be broken, in others they will have been skilfully manipulated. It is these idiosyncratic decisions that makes the built environment richer, but only when making good places remains the top design priority. The case studies have been chosen because they all perform well at an urban level, and their architecture is well appreciated. They show how quality can be realised in different ways. They are a small and diverse sample of projects, with a common thread of good place-making.

As the varied case studies suggest, there are many different models for good housing design – they do not all have to be the same. What they will all have in common is an aspiration to fulfil commonly held values, qualities and principles, along the lines of those discussed in Chapter 4. In their diversity the projects represent the fact that universal rules for housing cannot apply.

These case studies cannot represent all contextual challenges and eventualities. What they do show is how varied responses might be and how the 'rules' may be broken in many ways for various effects. Every project breaks rules. Its success depends on the level of understanding of the rule breaking and the skill with which the compromises are managed. But each will to a greater or lesser degree fulfil various values and qualities held in good currency, generating compromises and gains. In short, the investigation of these case studies reveals the precarious balancing act that is housing design.

It follows that the case studies will all have their own design agendas and responses, each with a particular emphasis, which will differ from the others. They are all very different to each other and should not necessarily be directly compared, not least because they have different physical, social, cultural and economic contexts. Each has a specific challenge and is successful in its resolution. However, each design agenda will follow the same logical order, starting with the most strategic design decisions, and ending with the more specific and detailed issues.

Before getting into the design agenda for each case study, there is a brief description of the project's *background*. This is followed by some *up front* information which outlines the quantitative attributes of the project. This is intended as an important description of the key elements and attributes of each project. They provide a quantitative context for the design issues that follow, and are presented as a series of facts, or 'givens', that could be used as an important checklist.

At the end of each case study there is a summary of its key successes in design terms.

Case studies

- Housing at Parc de Bercy (overall masterplan of approximately 514 apartments).

- Tango Housing, Bo01, Malmo, Sweden (27 apartments in an overall masterplan of 550 homes).

- Century Court, Cheltenham, UK (9 houses and 87 apartments).

- Palm Housing, Coin Street, London, UK (11 houses and 16 apartments).

- Housing in the Calle del Carme, Barcelona, Spain (28 apartments).

7

HOUSING AT PARC DE BERCY

Paris, France

Architects
Master planner: Jean-Pierre Buffi. Architects: Frank Hammoutene,
Fernando Montes, Yves Lion, & Chaix Morel, Dusapin &
Leclercq, Christian de Portzamparc, Henri Ciriani
Developer
City of Paris/SEMAEST
Completed
circa 1995

Unity and diversity – a real piece of town.

The housing in the new district of Bercy has a symbiotic relationship with the new park. The park is the key urban element, but it was conceived with the housing bordering it. This is not the only good relationship in the new Bercy: the masterplan provides synthesis between the housing and all elements of the public realm, a factor of the way the various architects' development parcels were assigned. The housing displays both coherence and variety through its collection of architects. This is not the work of one person, but it is also not a competition ground for the architects involved. The housing at Parc de Barcy displays an attitude towards design that is conducive to creating real pieces of town – real places for residents and visitors.

BACKGROUND

A new metropolitan strategy for Paris (that obsolete industrial areas to the east should be annexed to the city) saw the metamorphosis of the Bercy site on the right bank of the Seine. This district was formerly the site of wine warehouses in the east of Paris.

Jean-Pierre Buffi was asked to co-ordinate the regeneration of the new Bercy district, which was slowly emerging from the urban wasteland deserted by the wine industry. While industrial wasteland rarely offers more than a few scattered buildings on polluted land, the Bercy site offered a vast space together with a built inheritance (some of it reusable) and above all an exceptional landscape – over 500 tall trees, most of them plane trees spread randomly along a network of small streets shaped by the crossing of ranks of wine cellars.

The new district of Bercy is today articulated around the 13.5 ha rectangular park designed by Bernard Huet and Phillippe Raguin: it is bordered on the north side by the housing which Buffi was responsible for co-ordinating. The built development is positioned along the Rue de Pommard, with the defunct Frank Gehry cultural centre (now a cinema) at its head. Despite the amount of social housing required by the programme, the buildings present an impressive façade to the park.

Buffi put forward six 'rules' in order to maintain unity and diversity:

- *to create a general unity by entrusting to each architect not one side of a space but both, which would include the space between the buildings.*
- *to make the roofs liveable by placing 'villas' there.*
- *to create a duplex scale by laying out balconies at every other level.*
- *to create a unifying bond by means of the continuous balconies along the park façade, designed by Buffi, and all with black enamel coating.*
- *to use pale or white stone in the park façades and grey or darker stone in the transverse streets.*
- *to maximise the relationship between the buildings and the park.*

UP FRONT

Number of dwellings	Approximately 514.
Site area	1.5 or 15 ha (including the park).
Density	Approximately 330 dph excluding the park (building area only) and 34 dph including the park.
Access to public transport	Bercy is well served by a network of transport links – buses, metro, and trains.
Access to amenities	Shopping parade on Rue de Pommard and shops, schools and offices integrated into the scheme.
Parking	Underground parking – 1.5 spaces per dwelling on average.
Tenure	A mix of tenures comprising private housing, Prix Locatif Aide (social housing with help towards rent payment), and Prix Locatif Intermediare (social housing – medium price range).
Uses	Residentials, shops, schools, nursery schools, crèches and offices.
Building types	Apartment buildings.
Building heights	Eight or nine storeys.
Unit types	Apartments (some duplexes).
Circulation	Apartments are grouped around circulation cores (no deck access).
Disabled access	Lifts to all units.
Communal open space	All buildings have access to courtyards within the blocks for communal use.
Private/semi-private open space	All units overlooking the park, and most of the others, have balconies.

THE DESIGN AGENDA

Making connections

The plots are organised on a grid that is permeable for pedestrians. The grid integrates the blocks with the park on one side and the rest of the Bercy district on the other. The frequent links allow a choice of routes for pedestrians, and the traffic is managed: some streets are for pedestrian and emergency access only (the park side and transverse streets), while most vehicle access to parking is from the Rue de Pommard.

Right   *Movement network is strongly linked into the park*
Below   *Aerial view of the park and the housing blocks*

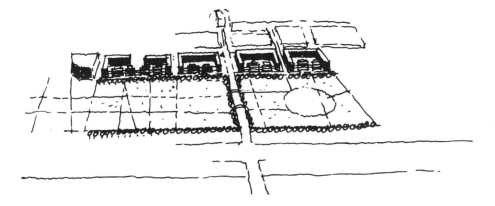

Providing green areas and corridors

The creation of a large park is central to the idea of the new Bercy. As the heart of the urban project the park suggested the positioning of the surrounding projects and the housing benefits from a long façade on the park. In contrast to the rigid urban structure that surrounds it, the park's identity is that of a mixed network of historic and contemporary patterns.

The park preserves the ancient paving of the old rail tracks that were used to move the wine to the banks of the Seine. This and the rows of trees, which have stood there for centuries, unveil the local memory. The park is divided into different parts providing a range of experiences – a kitchen garden, orchard or vineyard; a romantic garden arranged around a canal and lake with an island on which an ancient building has been left intact. On the edge closest to the Seine and the busy highway, the park is bordered by rows of lime trees to minimise noise impact.

Although large, the park provides intimacy and familiarity, in contrast to the urban vastness of the large historic and contemporary gardens of Paris. This invites interaction and use, and bonds the park to the housing. The park as the primary green element is visually and spatially linked to the housing courtyards and transverse streets.

Above   A rich landscape heritage
Right   Lake in the park

Arranging the built form – the Parisian context

Buffi based his ideas on the design of Parisian streets, using models of continuous street frontages as well as ones with gaps between plots, which would allow a visual permeability through to the park. Buffi accepted the prescribed size of the development plots without question. He did however attempt to create larger apertures from the development through to the park, giving the scheme a more modern style. He looked for a compromise between the closed Haussman-type plot and the 'modern block' where the internal space becomes the public space.

The built form is arranged as a succession of U's opening onto the park. Keeping three sides closed, Buffi created a transparent façade over the park by inserting isolated pavilions inside the U, linked by continuous balconies which filter the link between the courtyard and the park. The structure of the U is further broken down so that the legs or sides of the U are also seen as separate elements, allowing them to be grouped on either side of a street.

The gaps between the pavilions provide visual links into the courtyards and the buildings at the back of the U. At the same time the horizontal lines of the continuous balconies at every other level give grandeur to the park façade. Chaix & Morel's project emphasised these features by using double height glazed spaces giving the façade a more monumental scale than its neighbours, and the most striking feature, the metallic spiral of the penthouse at the top of the building which reflected Buffi's initial sketches for the roofs and the idea of 'urban houses' on the roof.

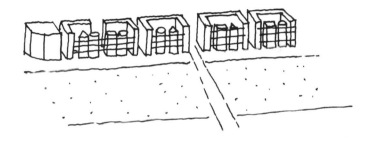

Left   *Gaps in the building provide visual links*
Right *U-shaped blocks and transparency over the park*

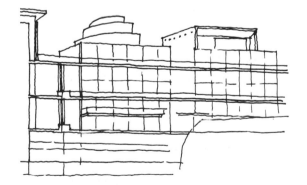

Left   *Gaps in the building provide visual links*
Right *Chaix & Morel's pavilions*

Defining public and private space

The device of breaking down the solidity of the park façade could have led to a blurring of the definition between public and private space. Fortunately this relationship is not compromised, as the courtyard space is still well defined by the building form, albeit with a degree of transparency, and access through the gaps of about 5 m is easy to control with visually permeable gates. This hybrid between the Hausmann and modern models is very effective – public and private space is strictly defined without compromising visual transparency.

Public and private space well defined

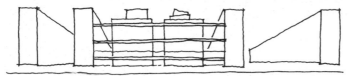

Public and private space well defined

Orienting active 'fronts' to the public realm

The central concept and key success of the Bercy housing is that of the highly positive relationship between the housing and the park. It is not only positive for the people living there, especially in units facing the park, but also for park users as the housing has enough mass and presence, without being dominating, to frame the park and make it feel safe and well overlooked. This surveillance is maximised with the glazed façades and balconies running along, and projecting from, the park façades.

All the streets or pedestrian routes – the park side promenade, the Rue de Pommard and the streets running between it and the park – accommodate the main entrances to the various buildings, thus orienting the activity to the public realm of the streets as well as the park.

Above   Balconies are well used and full of activity
Right   Buildings overlooking the park

Providing frequent and convenient access

Entrances to buildings are generally well defined. Ciriani's buildings are particularly successful as the entrances to the two buildings on either side of the street are directly opposite to each other and provide a transparency in an otherwise solid block, through to the respective courtyards beyond.

Other entrances from the promenade on the park façade are expressed as part of the 'gaps' in the built form, inviting visual and physical interaction between the courtyards and the public realm.

Left   *Entrances in gaps between buildings*
Above   *Entrance to one side of Ciriani's scheme*

Maximising positive aspect

The units facing the park have no lack of good aspect. The challenge for the architects was to provide the other units with aspect towards the park. They tackled this problem in various ways.

Ciriani's scheme consists of the sides of two U's facing onto a pedestrian street between the park and the Rue de Pommard. The flats overlooking the park are double volume with split internal levels, while living rooms in units overlooking the street have windows at an angle, jutting out and giving lateral views towards the park. This re-orientation of views from these apartments towards the park also helps avoid privacy being compromised between units facing each other across the narrow (11 m wide) street.

Hammoutene had to deal with a long main façade, badly oriented towards the massive blank wall of the Frank Gehry building. His response was to use cantilevered bow windows and continuous balconies with oversized railings.

By adopting this open, permeable façade he exploited the lateral views towards the park.

Above   *View of Ciriani's scheme from the park*
Right   *Plan of Ciriani's project*
Below   *Hammoutene's scheme exploits lateral views*

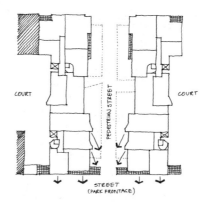

COURT

PEDESTRIAN STREET

COURT

STREET
(PARK FRONTAGE)

Encouraging unity and variety

Apart from Buffi's brief to come up with an urban design strategy for the site, he was also charged with finding a way of combining unity with diversity. Buffi referred to street models that incorporated a mixed architectural expression. But he also wanted to incorporate the linking elements in the form of continuous balconies from other street models. He tried, with success, to marry nostalgia for the historic town and modernism by asking the architects to work under a set of rules towards a traditional urban approach dressed in modernism.

Buffi tried to find a solution to the issue of encouraging diversity while maintaining a coherence to the overall scheme. His method of breaking the form up into spaces, blocks and pavilions proved successful. Each architect was given plots either facing each other across a street or on opposite sides of a courtyard space. Buffi then added rules about the building form. He did not want to impose too strong a design 'code' as to hinder creativity or prevent future changes. However, he did put down some basic principles about size, roofs, depth of balconies and height limitations. He also wanted to maintain the transparency within the built form. This led to a requirement for the façades along the park to be 70% glazed, while the façades along the streets only had to be 30% glazed. This, combined with the fact that the side streets did not require the more expensive light-coloured stone necessary for the park façades, made the buildings framing the streets cheaper to build. This allowed the integration of less expensive social housing units.

Despite these provisions for less expensive units within the overall project, each architect worked under very strict rules and it is difficult to distinguish between social and market housing, or to easily attribute buildings to any architect in particular.

Strong building expression defines the street corner

Pavilions on the park frontage are expressed

Development parcels for legible streets

One of the key successes of this scheme, which involved several architects, is that development parcels were assigned so that one architect designed two buildings on either side of a street or space, whereas usually development parcels are packaged around blocks. The approach at Bercy makes a significant contribution to the legibility of the streets, only falling down at the end where the housing meets the blank side façade of Frank Gehry's American Centre, which has since closed and become a cinema.

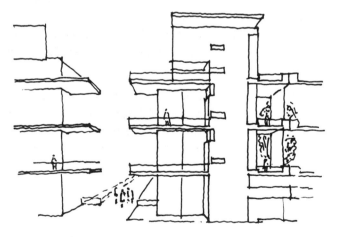

Left   Ciriani's buildings frame the street
Right   The park façade gives legibility to the street through its common elements

SUMMARY OF SUCCESSES

- *This masterplan was designed for a variety of architects, but ensured that there was cohesion among the various designs – the result is not a scheme or project, but a series of buildings and spaces that form a cohesive 'piece of town'.*

- *The big gesture of the park is matched by the housing. The required high density also gave the park a necessary strong and defining edge. The park and the buildings complement each other.*

- *The concentration of buildings against the expanse of the park gives the scheme impact, status, and most importantly, quality amenity space for all residents and visitors to the area.*

- *The masterplan allowed for a mix of private and social housing without any distinction being made between the various buildings – they were all part of an overall framework that prioritised frontage onto the streets and parks. This allowed the different buildings to be accessed directly from the public realm.*

- *A key success is the fine balance that was struck between transparency and definition of the housing blocks. Although they function very well as perimeter blocks, making clear distinctions between public and private space, they remain visually permeable, maintaining links with the park.*

8

TANGO HOUSING
AT Bo01

Malmo, Sweden

Architects
Moore Ruble Yudell Architects and Planners
(Santa Monica, California) in association with
Bertil Ohrstrom of FFNS Arkitekter AB (Malmo)
Completion
2001
Developers/client
MKB Fastighets AB

The Bo01 project is an exemplar scheme of environmental and ecological sustainability. But with all the bells and whistles, social sustainability has been compromised. Is this kind of sustainability sustainable, or do we have to wait and see?

As a showcase project, one cannot help wonder if Bo01 is just another icon in the name of sustainability. With all its beautiful landscaping and ecological systems, the homes on offer are only available to a very exclusive market. Although there is a variety of home procurement options, all the housing is exceptionally expensive, with very high service charges. However, almost all the houses have been sold. There is clearly a market for this kind of housing, and a common argument is that it is a legitimate market as it brings the wealthy back into the city and out of the suburbs.

Hopefully the future will see a reduction in premiums for good environmental design as these initiatives become more mainstream. And hopefully the future will also value well-designed housing that does not necessarily glitter. Only time will tell whether Bo01 can be socially sustainable. But this does not detract from the project's offer of a valuable and rich palette of design choices for energy saving and ecological sensitivity.

Looking at Bo01 in its most positive light, and focusing on the Tango Housing as a particular example, the emphasis should be on the approach to design, and this approach can be adopted to deliver equally positive spaces without the expense that has been incurred on this project, because it is primarily about the relationships between the buildings. At Bo01 a new city is conceived not as a collection of buildings with the bits in between landscaped, but rather in a multi-dimensional way. The design philosophy at Bo01 embraces a combination of green environmental values and urban place making, integrated landscaping and good design at every level. These agendas do not compete with each other but rather reinforce a holistic approach. Physical place-making becomes all the more powerful when conceived in these terms.

BACKGROUND

Bo01 (City of Tomorrow) is the first phase of a long-term development plan for the Vastra Hamnen (Western Harbour) area in Malmo. A European Housing Exposition, Bo01 is sited on a post-industrial waterfront site within walking distance of both the city centre and the beach. The project is expected to become a driving force in Mamo's overall development as a sustainable city. It is also expected to be a model for the reclamation of industrial harbour sites. The Tango Housing project was one of the housing schemes as part of Bo01.

The shaping of the overall plan for Bo01, which called for housing surrounded by parkland and the sea, is described by the Principal Exposition Architect, Klas Tham in terms of the goals of the design team:

> To offer an urban structure that is sufficiently robust, to meet the demands of an uncertain future (the network structure of the block city and clear borders between public and private spaces); to provide the conditions for the essence of the city, the meeting between different people and cultures; to come about gradually (the small-scale property division of the plan, its range of different residential environments); to let cars through, but on the terms of the pedestrians; to provide the conditions of a city environment which, over and above empathy and comprehensibility, also offer a wealth of information, mystery, surprises, and many unique and promising urban spaces; a dramatic tension between the grand and the intimate; to offer a wealth of all forms of vegetation, from the individual garden, to the sheltered, thickly wooded public canal park through the interior of the area. That is how the plan took shape.

> The grid has been distorted by the wind, among other things, like a fishnet hung out to dry. As a result it has actually become more rational, more valuable to build, live and stroll around in. Thus the urban form is not from the 'Middle Ages' but is of today. The inspiration comes from antiquity, the Middle Ages, the Renaissance, the Baroque period, the 20th century; and the scale of the interior of the area takes its

*precedents from typical northern European cities – low, tight, intimate,
incredibly efficient in its use of area.*

From Bo01 City of Tomorrow, Vastra Hamnen, Malmo, Sweden

http://home.att.net/~amcnet/bo01.html

A 'quality programme' was developed by the city to help achieve the goals set for Bo01 and to define minimum standards for participating developers and builders. The programme sets guidelines for architectural qualities, choice of materials, energy consumption, green issues and technical infrastructure.

Eighteen property developers and 22 different architecture firms were involved in the design and development of about 550 dwellings of various types in the first phase of Bo01. The area is characterised by diversity. The site shows a multitude of architectural solutions that go hand in hand with innovative measures for renewable energy supply and increased biodiversity.

The lack of management of style or any design coding has an interesting effect, with the only coherence between the buildings being due to the family of heights and colours, and the emphasis on quality public realm. In some cases it is disappointing to find two vastly different architectural treatments jostling against each other, where relationships between buildings are less than complementary. However it works, mostly, with a richness, variety and texture that would be difficult to achieve with design guidance at the more prescriptive end of the scale.

UP FRONT

Number of dwellings	27 apartments in the Tango building.
Site area	0.17 ha.
Density	The density of the Tango building is 158 dph.
	The average density over the whole Bo01 area, which is a mix of houses and apartments, is expected to be 72 dph when fully developed.
Access to public transport	As with the whole area, pedestrians and cyclists have priority. Bus stops are within 300 m from dwellings, running at 7-min intervals and connecting with several main central points in town which is a short distance away.
Access to amenities	There are currently only a few shops and restaurants in Bo01, but the mix of uses in the area is growing. This is the target area for all new projects in Malmo and there is an overall masterplan to link the area to the city.
Parking	The Tango Building does not have dedicated parking in the basement, as do some of the other buildings in Bo01. It does provide easily accessible parking for 2 cycles/unit.
	Bo01 is primarily a pedestrian priority site. Cars are let through but on the pedestrians' terms. Parking of residents' cars is in designated parking areas outside the housing area itself or in underground parking areas within the Bo01 area. Parking was planned at 0.7 spaces per dwelling but this has been problematic for the residents who can afford higher levels of car ownership. Temporary parking has been provided, in the vicinity of the old SAAB factory nearby, to accommodate the excess requirements. As soon as the new multi-storey car park has been built, the parking area will be moved there.
	The car pool that was planned did not come to fruition due to lack of interest.
Tenure	The Tango apartments are rented.

Generally Bo01 has a mix of rental, private and co-operatively owned housing. Sweden does not provide social housing, rather housing allowances are used to help families that are less equipped to pay housing costs, irrespective of tenure form.

Uses

Residential with some ground floor units adaptable to become shops.

Building types

Apartment building,

Building heights

Three to six storeys.

Unit types

The units in Tango range from studio apartments ($55\,m^2$) to three bed apartments ($181\,m^2$).

Generally Bo01 has a mix of apartments and terraced and detached houses.

Circulation

There are four circulation cores, each with a lift and a staircase. Each core serves 2 or 3 units per floor.

Disabled access

Access for disabled is available for all apartments. There is level access from the street to lifts in all cases, even when the ground floor level is higher than the street level in which case the lift continues down to the street level.

Refuse disposal

Kitchen sinks have food waste disposers and there is a centralised vacuum waste chute system. In the food waste disposer the organic waste is ground and disposed in separate pipes to an underground collector tank. From there the sludge is taken to an underground collector tank and then to a biogas plant together with other organic waste. Through anaerobic digestion the organic waste is transformed to biogas that can be used as fuel or to produce heat and electricity.

Recycling

There is an easily accessible waste separation room in the basement and in the entrance pavilion.

Communal open space	The building encloses a central communal garden.
Private/semi-private open space	All apartments have a small patio or balcony.
Landscape and 'green' features	The landscape concept is fully integrated with the building design. The central courtyard is divided into distinct parts including an 'uncultivated' marsh landscape of reeds and grasses, which is fed by recycled rainwater through man-made streams and a pond. In addition:

- Underground pollutants were extracted with several species decontaminating plants.
- The flat roof surfaces are covered with grass to restore oxygen to the atmosphere.
- Rainwater from roofs is recycled and used to irrigate water gardens.
- Run-off water from all surfaces is directed into a perimeter channel and then taken to a central cistern for the whole area and cleaned. The cleaned water is then directed to the ocean.

These features are common to many of the Bo01 projects, but the various green spaces vary in their appearance. Each is laid out according to a points system which gives a higher grade for 'greener' features. For example a tree or water feature counts for more points than a square metre of grass — this system has encouraged variety in the gardens. It is a requirement that landscape architects are engaged at the beginning of each project.

Energy saving measures	Tango features the following energy saving measures, some of which have been used throughout the Bo01 project:

- Large areas of the roof surfaces have photovoltaic panels which provide heating and cooling for the building. The solar cells produce more than 100% of the building's energy needs. The excess energy is sold back to Southern Sweden's electric company (Sydkraft) and then sent back via district heating.

— All the glass areas on the building are triple glazed to provide insulation. The outside layer contains transparent argon gas. Air is warmed as it passes the argon layer on its way to warm the interior.
— The 'intelligent wall' that runs through the building, through each unit, supports all power and data cabling and allows users to monitor their usage of energy resources through computerised systems. Residents can monitor security, deliveries and energy consumption, order services, or adjust their thermostats from long distance.

Management and maintenance

Gardens are designed for minimal maintenance. The building is managed by MKB Fastighets AB who have an office on the Bo01 site. There is a concierge/caretaker on the Tango premises every day. These services are covered by charges paid by residents.

THE DESIGN AGENDA

Making connections

The Tango building is arranged on a city block site within the overall masterplan of the Bo01 area, which is organised around a loosely structured grid of streets. This permeable network provides a choice of routes for pedestrians, and connects homes to facilities and amenities.

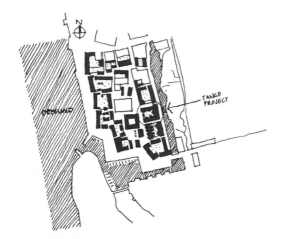

Tango building in the Bo01 context

Aerial view of Bo01

Providing green areas and corridors

The residential area of Bo01 is a loose grid of structures built around courtyards of varying scale and character. These courtyards and spaces form a green network linked to each other and the sea by a series of open channels and ponds.

The central courtyard in the Tango project is part of this overall concept for Bo01, linking in with a network of green corridors and spaces in the Bo01 area. It is a core concept of the Tango project itself, and was conceived of as strongly as the buildings.

Above   *Green elements in the public realm*
Right   *Tango's central courtyard*

Defining public and private space

The building's form as a perimeter block creates a very strong distinction between public and private space. The exterior of the block provides a bold edge to the public realm, while the interior of the block surrounding the green courtyard has a softer and more intimate form. The block is 'solid' on three sides, while the fourth western side breaks down in scale.

This arrangement of buildings and space is a deliberate echo of the overall masterplan. The masterplan concept was to have a very strong edge to the project area, with taller and more formally arranged buildings around its perimeter, and the buildings in the interior 'dissolving' and becoming more loosely or informally arranged. Accordingly, Tango's perimeter block form is fragmented on the western side, the gaps in the building form allowing views into the courtyard. This transparency does not compromise the enclosure and security of the courtyard or the distinction between public and private space. In the same way, transparency at the various entrance points in the overall perimeter block form does not compromise enclosure of space and definition of public and private. In fact, it provides interest for passers-by and an impression of activity – a relationship is established between the building and its neighbouring space.

Built form arrangement

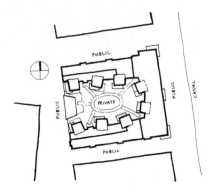

Orienting active 'fronts' to the public realm

All entrances to the building are from the street (public realm) sides of the building, which perform well as 'fronts'. Entrances are clearly defined and welcoming and are well articulated in the façade. While these 'front' façades are of a much more urban expression than those of the buoyant interior, there is a liberal distribution of windows and bay windows to enliven them.

Above Entrance to apartments
Right Frontage onto the street

Providing frequent and convenient access

Access arrangements are very successful. The ideal scenario in a perimeter block or courtyard arrangement such as this is for the circulation cores to be accessible from the street (keeping activity on the street) as well as from the central amenity area (allowing each unit access to the communal space). This scheme takes this arrangement one step further by providing an entrance pavilion that allows glimpses into the courtyard and at the same time protects the privacy and security of the interior of the scheme. This multi-layered access arrangement gives the scheme fluidity, offering choice and convenience, while maintaining the integrity and security of the private spaces within.

The street entrances allow disabled access as the lifts are accessible from the entrance level as well as the 'ground' or garden level which is a few steps higher. The lifts also access all the storage facilities in the basement.

The number of street entrances is very much a factor of the layout of the units. In this case the cores each access a cluster of 2 or 3 units per floor, necessitating several street entrances. This arrangement of units and access also allows a degree of personalisation of the lobby spaces as few units share the space.

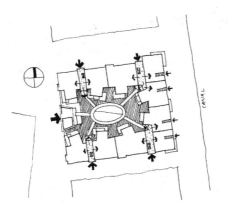

Access into and through the building

Responding to the context – expression

No overall code for the design of façades was prescribed for the Bo01 area. The aim was to provide an abundance of expressions. The city specified a basic colour scheme: pale façades facing the sea and canal, and more colour towards the inner areas. The external façades of the Tango project are intended to respond to the urban nature of the perimeter of the Bo01 scheme. This is achieved with a contemporary interpretation of traditional board and batten construction, the louvred panels giving the façades texture, providing subtle reflections of light and presenting a discreet street presence.

Variety within the Tango building itself is a key feature, and executed in a very considered way, allowing the flexibility and variety not to be in competition with the overall coherence of the scheme. The variety is present in the vibrantly colourful towers in the courtyard with their various angles and colours and heights, and visible from the inner areas of Bo01 scheme. These towers 'dance' around the west-facing garden (hence the name Tango, which is also a play on the design partnership between the American and Swedish architects). With distant views of the Oresund Sound at higher levels, the living room of each unit occupies part of a tower, projecting inwards into the garden.

Above *External façade treatment on the canal frontage*
Right *Strong urban exterior and softer varied forms in the interior*
Below *Visual links into the courtyard*

Responding to context – scale and massing

The massing of the structures in the Bo01 plan is designed to be sensitive to the windy nature of the site, with the buildings serving as wind-breaks as well as sheltering arms to the more closed and intimate spaces within the area. Tall buildings on the outskirts form a wind shelter around a smaller scale and green interior.

The built form of the Tango block again responds excellently to the differing environments met by each side of the block, and fits in with the overall massing strategy of the masterplan which is to grade the scale down from the edges of the scheme towards the interior.

The edge facing the canal is the highest, maximising the good aspect over the canal, while the edge facing the interior is the lowest. The building heights grade down from the canal to a more intimate scale at the internal street.

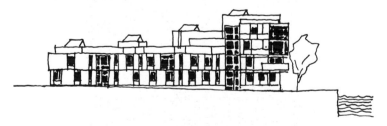

Changing levels and massing

Accommodating the possibility of future uses

A useful feature of the Bo01 area is its gentle mounding from the centre of the site down to the sea or canal. In the case of the Tango building, which has a consistent 'ground floor' level, this means that the floor to ceiling heights on the ground floor apartments facing the canal are very high.

It is an aspiration of the masterplan to have other activities along the canal edge. The present arrangement is that the floors of these apartments are raised to a suitable residential level (the same as all other ground floor apartments). Access to these apartments is either up stairs from the street, or via the circulation cores.

This gives the potential for the ground floor apartments on the canal side to be converted to shops at a later stage. This eventuality will go a long way to increasing ground floor activity along the canal front.

Above Entrances to ground floor units enabling flexible uses
Right Canal frontage suitable for other uses

Providing a range of outdoor communal and semi-private spaces

The architects designed the outdoor courtyard or 'Yard' as a metaphor of an island wetland through its formal design and planting. Oriented towards the west, the central mound or 'island' is a place where residents can gather formally or informally. This central outdoor space is linked by individual footbridges to the residential circulation cores over a marshy vegetation lush with reeds and perennials.

Apart from its ecological benefits, the marsh vegetation is a vital factor in the overall success of the central space:

— The reeds provide a semi-transparent screen between the communal 'island' and the semi-private ground floor patios.
— The effect on the eye and ear is very pleasant and gives the courtyard the feel of a soft oasis, very much in contrast to the urban streets and squares outside. The sound of water is soothing and this quality is shared with the outside world – passers by can also hear it and they can glimpse through the fence railings and reed screens into the abundant and verdant space.

Above   Communal amenity space in the courtyard
Below   Semi-private balconies and patios

Each apartment is also provided with a semi-private patio or balcony. The balconies and patios are comfortably shallow as their space can easily integrate with the apartments through large glazed sliding doors. On the ground floor, where privacy would be most compromised, the distinction between inside and outside is barely noticeable as the reed screening becomes the edge of the space.

Managing privacy and surveillance

This building is a great example of getting the balance between privacy and surveillance right. This is the happy result of a holistic design approach where the communal and semi-private or private spaces were designed in tandem rather than as separate entities. The flow between the spaces is seamless where it needs to be, while the need for privacy is not compromised. The central court is completely overlooked, and while one could feel that the large expanses of glass would take surveillance to an unhappy extreme and/or compromise privacy, the reflectiveness of the glazing maintains a film of privacy during the day, and at night the white blinds built into the glazing system allow the building to glow like a series of lanterns. Individuality of each unit becomes particularly apparent at night where each unit uses the blinds to a varying degree.

Surveillance is at its best in the courtyard as the predominant spaces overlooking it are living rooms. In terms of privacy, living rooms are the least likely to be compromised by being too close to the communal space.

Reeds provide screening for patios

Using interfaces and thresholds effectively

A very successful device used throughout Bo01 is the open water channels that drain run-off water to the canal or sea. These channels are attractively designed with a paving trim and stone features. As they are placed alongside the building edges, they create a 'buffer' zone between the building and the street/walkway. This is important as most of the bedrooms are located on the street façades, and have a need for privacy. Because the natural ground level drops relative to the internal ground level which remains consistent, passers-by will generally not be looking directly into the private rooms. As an added precaution, the lower panels of the full-height windows are semi-opaque.

On the northern side of the building, the street or space between buildings is wider, allowing space for a planted bed between the building and street, increasing the buffer zone particularly at the western end of the building where the natural ground level is almost the same as the internal ground floor unit level.

Open channels along building thresholds

SUMMARY OF SUCCESSES

- *The whole Bo01 project is exemplary in its approach to environmental sustainability.*

- *In urban design terms the Tango project's key success is its clear distinction between public and private space.*

- *The integrated landscape concept allows a strong contrast between the urban street, and the soft and intimate central courtyard space.*

- *Landscaping provides privacy to patios opening onto the court, while surveillance over the space is maintained.*

- *In the Tango project there is frequent access from the public realm into the building, keeping activity on the external street. The cores run through into the courtyard space which also has its own access from the street. This gives residents maximum choice and permeability.*

- *The potential for ground floor units along the canal to adapt into shops in the future is a key sustainability feature.*

9

CENTURY COURT

Cheltenham, England

Architects
Feilden Clegg Bradley
Developers
Crest Nicholson
Completed
2001

Responding to context is what this scheme does to the full. It has a different expression for each of its neighbours, creating a variety of rich spaces around and within. With its street-based variety, this is a piece of town rather than a building with a single identity. This is not to the detriment of architectural statement-making: lovers of iconic gestures will agree that this 'fine-grain' response does not compromise the scheme's boldness in the face of a sensitive and historic setting.

BACKGROUND

On a highly sensitive site near the centre of Cheltenham, Century Court shows that a modern design approach for high-density living can enhance a historic setting. This brave and new approach demonstrates a public acceptance of and desire for new, innovative and bold design in a historic setting (70% of units were sold before the scheme was completed).

This project also proves that high density and high quality can and should live happily together. This at a time when pastiche cookie-cutter schemes were being churned out by volume house-builders. Providing accommodation that would otherwise have probably been located on an edge of town site, a high-density solution was required to create a high-value site, which was suitable for competing with more suburban executive housing solutions. Achieving a high density was not only important for the commercial viability of the development: there was a strong need to create a suitably urban block. This coupled with a highly respected developer with a brave new aesthetic was a recipe for success.

This project is significant both as a residential development on brownfield land, and in terms of its extremely sensitive position in a conservation area and opposite the Grade II listed buildings of Cheltenham College on Bath Road, near the centre of Cheltenham. The site was formerly occupied by an undistinguished 1960s office block with extensive parking. With the development of private housing on this highly sensitive site, a new and more appropriate, if contentious life has been injected to the site and its immediate surrounds.

UP FRONT

Number of dwellings	87 apartments and 9 town houses (96 total).
Site area	0.9 ha.
Density	106 dph.
Access to public transport	Bus routes on Bath Road. Train station about a 20-min walk.
Access to amenities	This is not a central location – there are a few local amenities and central Cheltenham is a short bus ride away.
Parking	Lower than 1.5 per unit – 121 spaces (intended as one space per unit and the remainder as visitors' parking). Parking was reduced to nearly half its normal standard for this kind of housing. Incorporating it into the basement of the scheme helped overcome some of the inherent problems of high-density development. However, the parking originally intended for residents parking has been sold to residents, leaving no visitors' parking available. Visitors' parking is now an issue that is dealt with by the management company. The basement parking is well designed as a useable and safe place with permanent lighting.

There is a cycle parking zone for residents in the basement. |
Tenure	Private sale.
Uses	Residential and a small private gymnasium.
Building types	Houses and apartment buildings.
Building heights	Three, four and five storeys.
Unit types	Houses, flats and penthouses.
Circulation	Houses have their own entrances off the street, and apartments are accessed from circulation cores serving mostly two apartments per floor.

Disabled access	Access for the disabled is from the lifts in the basement parking. Level access from the courtyard was not a regulatory requirement at the time.
Refuse disposal	There are bin areas in the basement parking. Refuse is brought up for disposal once a week by the management company.
Recycling	No requirement at the time from the planning authority.
Communal open space	The central courtyard is a communal area and provides limited recreational space.
Private/semi-private open space	Gardens and roof terraces for houses, balconies for apartments.
Energy saving measures	Simple energy saving measures included the compact planning and high levels of fabric insulation, ensuring high-standard assessment procedures (SAP) ratings and consequent lower energy consumption.
Management and maintenance	Home-owners pay for a management company that attends to maintenance and management issues.

THE DESIGN AGENDA

Making connections

The site forms part of a larger street block with streets on three sides connecting up with the urban grid. This urban grid is reinforced by the development, which fronts onto the previously ill-defined streets and public spaces.

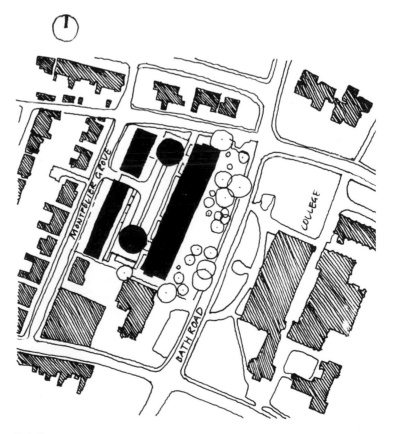

The buildings in context

Providing green areas and corridors

The compulsory setback of the buildings from Bath Road leaves a substantial 'green' space in front of the buildings – a grassed area with a range of mature specimen trees. This can be seen as a 'buffer' between the building and the busy Bath Road.

The space has been made into a positive element that is very visually pleasing for residents and passers-by. For reasons discussed later, it has also missed a few opportunities to be a more alive and integrated feature of the project.

Green space between the building and Bath Road

Arranging the built forms – public and private

The buildings are laid out in a variation of the traditional perimeter block with two parallel 100 m long terraces and two drums at each end abutting the terraces and defining the central courtyard. This is not a literal perimeter block but performs the same purpose with a strict definition of inside and outside, public and private. The use of the drums at each end instead of closing the blocks off completely allows glimpses into the central courtyard. These views through are an appropriate scale to create a sense of enclosure and definition of the internal courtyard, without inviting entry or compromising security.

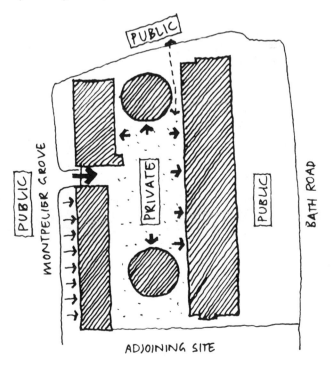

Built form arrangement showing entrances

Orienting active fronts to the public realm

Perimeter blocks are particularly effective when their form not only encloses a central space, distinguishing between public and private, but when it is taken a step further so that all front entrances are on the outside, the public realm is enlivened and it has a more widely spread impact: the streets or public spaces are imbued with more activity, and choice for residents is increased as their access to the outside world is direct.

In this case, the entrances are not on the public side of the buildings, apart from the houses where the access is directly off the street. Most entrances are from within the central court. This does make the development into a semi-gated 'community'. However, the scheme does not suffer too much from this as the aspect is right – the buildings' primary aspect (living rooms) is always to the outside, overlooking and fronting onto the public realm – street on one side and park on the other. While the park suffers from a lack of activity generated by the building it has no lack of surveillance from the numerous and generous balconies overlooking it.

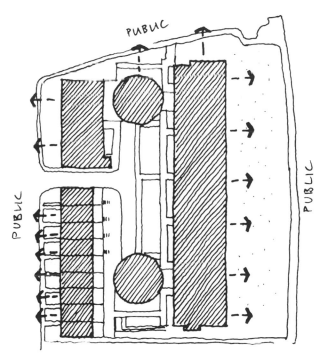

Above Houses fronting onto the street
Right Main aspect is towards the public realm
Below Apartments overlooking the park

Providing frequent and easy points of access

The front doors of the houses are on the street side and they have access to their back doors from the basement parking and central court via their back gardens. The rest of the buildings are accessed via the courtyard. There is one point of vehicular access which takes cars into the court and down into the basement parking. Pedestrian access to the court is at two points, one via the vehicular entrance and the other via the pedestrian entrance on the side street.

This controlled access was part of the attractiveness of the scheme for buyers. However, this design decision, while maintaining security and control within the scheme, compromises the choice of residents and the ease with which they can make use of the beautifully maintained park in front of the building on the Bath Road side. It is a pity that the entrances do not go through the block, at least at ground level to make more of a physical connection with the green space. This would not compromise privacy of residents as the building 'floats' above the park space to ventilate the parking basement below.

Access to the apartments from the central court is frequent and well defined, with two to four units sharing circulation cores. There is also access to each core from the basement parking. This relationship between the buildings and the courtyard enlivens the space, and gives it a character one might expect from a terraced street.

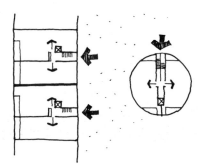

Typical access arrangements from the court

Responding to context – scale and massing

The scale and massing of the buildings carefully reduces their scale and impact on the surrounding urban form.

The western boundary of the site is smaller in scale with early Victorian villas on the opposite side of the street. The town houses facing this residential street are three storeys, but the ground levels and storey heights make them appear to be of the same scale as the two-storey houses opposite. Their regular entrances also give the terrace a rhythm appropriate to the street. This element of the scheme has a finer 'grain' of development, with an appropriately smaller scale and rhythm of houses.

The five-storey terrace at the front facing Bath Road is of a much grander scale, in proportion to the college on the other side of the road, and reflecting the scale of the white stucco villas along Bath Road. From a proportion point of view, this grand terrace is not as articulated as the villas: it reads as one building which could be argued as appropriate considering its dialogue with the college building across the road. The top or fifth floor with its 'pop-up' volumes is set back beneath the roof to reduce the impact of its scale. The parapet level of adjacent buildings on Bath Road determined the height of the building.

The two circular villa blocks at each end and the remaining villa block on the residential street are all four storeys, which is in keeping with the ambient building heights in the area.

Concept sketch by the architects

Responding to context – varied form and expression

A central challenge facing the architects was finding an architectural language compatible with and potentially uniting the diverse architecture surrounding the site.

A key success of this building is the varied response of each form to its edge or context. Each façade has a different expression, in particular the two long terraces which respond in turn to their very different edges of quiet residential street and busy main road with listed college buildings.

With the encouragement and support of the planning authority to submit a contemporary design, the architects sought to complement the scale and massing of the surrounding urban block with an uncompromisingly modern interpretation of a Regency Terrace along the key elevation on Bath Road. The result is a building with a calm grace – contemporary but respectful – a building that can live on comfortably as a counterpoint and friend to the college building.

This Bath Road façade is also cut away to provide generous balconies, described as outdoor rooms, for each apartment, and wonderful views to the city and countryside beyond. The subject of much debate about architectural appropriateness, this building with its cool modernism is in direct contrast to the college. But together they create a formal avenue along Bath Road, each performing its part without compromising the other.

The houses on the residential street are quietly assertive, maintaining a presence in the street while contributing to its rhythm. The frequent entrances, the modulation of the façades and the double-volume spaces expressed in the elevation give life to the street in a cool and reflective way. This terrace of houses uses the same crisp white externally insulated render system which makes reference to the pale stucco façades of Regency Cheltenham, while also giving good thermal performance to the building envelope.

The 'drums' and the interior of the court see the introduction of hardwood cladding which sits very comfortably next to the sparkling white render, and is complemented by the crisp grey aluminium window sections. The co-ordinated colours and textures combine to create a modernism suited to its context, restrained while making its mark on the urban landscape.

Above Bath Road façade
Right Houses accessed from the residential street
Below College building on the other side of Bath Road

Managing privacy and personalisation

In most cases, issues of privacy and overlooking are controlled or managed by the arrangement of rooms within units. A potential pinch-point in this scheme is in the proximity between the circular villa blocks and the buildings on either side of them. This is probably less of a problem where the houses abut the villas, and the villas have been designed so that their primary aspects are to the front and back rather than the sides. This prevents overlooking and privacy problems but the access to daylight in some of the bedrooms of the terraces could be compromised.

The Bath Road façade works exceptionally well with its multi-layered quality creating a series of indoor–outdoor spaces. The balconies are very well used, and the glass balustrades provide a layer of reflectiveness that gives the building coherence despite the personalisation of each of these balcony spaces. This personalisation with its sheen of reflectivity gives the building an overall richness and character without compromising the integrity of the façade.

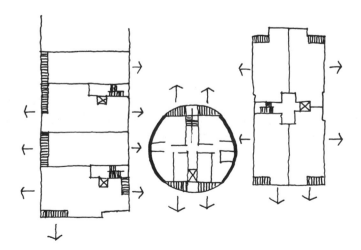

Left Arranging rooms and windows to manage privacy
Below Pinch-point between buildings

Managing parking and quality amenity space

The central court was designed not to accommodate cars — all cars are placed underneath the buildings in a naturally ventilated basement. However, the access area to the parking can be found to have a liberal sprinkling of cars, probably due to the fact that all visitors' parking has been sold off to apartment owners. (This demand is due to the relatively low parking provision. It was a breakthrough to achieve such a high density without the scheme being dominated by parking. By cutting the normal standard for car parking by about half, the scheme made a powerful statement about the type of people it was confident it would attract.)

The opportunity offered by the enclosure of space and the placement of cars in the basement seems to have been lost in the landscape offered in the central court. The access to the parking is through the court; hence the ramps and driveways to two separate accesses dominate and divide the space, especially with incidental parking along the access ways. Although the remaining landscaping is attractive and well maintained, it leaves little space for informal or formal social use.

Central court accommodates access to basement parking

In contrast, the park on Bath Road provides a wonderful front drop to the building. It is particularly attractive due to the time, effort and resources invested in maintaining and enhancing it. This may not be the case in projects without substantial service charges. However, it has missed an opportunity to become a well-used space, rather than just a space for residents of the block to look over from their balconies. This lack of use is distinctly related to the lack of access directly between the building and the park.

Meeting the ground – interfaces and thresholds

The main terrace is slightly raised to allow ventilation to the basement parking below. This has also been used as a privacy device that has its success in the actual height by which the building has been raised. If it was too high, the interface with the building would be dominated by the ventilation grills and would be alienating to the passer-by. If it was too low, passers-by would be able to see into the apartments. This level varies with the ground level but at an average of 500 mm above ground it works very well, striking the balance between privacy in the home and activity and surveillance for the passer-by.

The relationship between the backs of the houses and the court is less happy but this is more to do with the height and choice of fencing material than the arrangement of the spaces. The back gardens are raised affording them a level of privacy that could allow lower and less intrusive fences. While the confusion between backs and fronts is overcome in the main terrace by high-quality design and good aspect, the backs of the houses look distinctly like backs and slightly sour the flavour of the central court. This is not a big issue here as security measures are strong enough for this kind of interface not to encourage anti-social behaviour as it may in a less controlled environment. This model should not be used for less well-resourced projects.

Above   Main terrace raised to ventilate the basement
Below   Back gardens interface with the central court

SUMMARY OF SUCCESSES

- *This scheme's primary success lies in its response to context — from a graceful modern interpretation of the Regency Terrace as a counterpoint to the listed college building on the other side of the road, to the fine-grain expression of the terrace houses in harmony with and accessed from the residential street. The scheme does not read as one building with four sides, but rather a series of buildings that face and enhance the three urban streets.*

- *The building facing Bath Road enjoys a very positive relationship with the park space in front of it, despite the fact that there is no direct access from the apartments into the park. The primary aspect of all apartments is towards the park and the façade is layered with glazing and balconies, ensuring that the park is well overlooked.*

- *The ground floor of the building had to be raised to allow for ventilation of the basement parking. This created a very successful threshold condition where the privacy of ground floor apartments was protected. At the same time, the level change was not so big as to present a blank wall on the ground level, which would have been negative for pedestrians outside the building.*

10

PALM HOUSING

Coin Street, London, UK

Architect
Lifschutz Davidson
Developer
Coin Street Community Builders
Completed
1994

A success story for Coin Street Community Builders (CSCB) – The Palm Housing project offers flexible accommodation, co-op tenure and management, and an attractive and bold double fronted building as a mediator between important public spaces.

A beacon of good architecture in central London, the Palm Housing project presents a crisp and lively face to its less than distinguished urban backdrop. But the success of this project is not only about good urbanism. The building form is also a result of a great deal of discussion with the local community, and the flexibility offered by the homes is an indication of the architects' understanding of changing family needs.

The project presented interesting urban challenges, especially in terms of public and private space. The very narrow site forced the architects to pay attention to subtle transitions and interfaces between public and private, form and space. While the building stands proud in the riverside context as an example of quality high-density housing, it is its edges and interfaces that mark its real success in urban design terms.

BACKGROUND

In 1984 residents in Waterloo and north Southwark formed CSCB as a not-for-profit company. This followed years of opposition to various speculative proposals for the area. Coin Street Secondary Housing Co-operative (CSS) – a legally separate housing association – was established to develop housing sites acquired on a 125-year lease from CSCB. CSCB is one of Britain's most successful community development enterprises, dedicated to building affordable housing and meeting other community needs on its London South Bank site.

Following the less successful first housing scheme, CSCB decided to raise the calibre of future schemes by awarding commissions on the basis of limited architectural competitions. The Palm Housing project is the first scheme awarded in this way and has been met with resounding success. It has been followed by the equally successful Iroko Housing project, which follows a traditional street pattern and forms a perimeter block making clear distinctions between public and private space. The reason for the focus here on the Palm Housing project is due to its response to the challenges of a much more constrained and demanding site, and its important place-making role for the wider Coin Street and riverside area.

UP FRONT

Number of dwellings	11 houses, 16 apartments.
Site area	0.15 ha (excluding public park).
Density	180 dph (excluding public park).
Access to public transport	Excellent. Waterloo station and several bus routes within easy access.
Access to amenities	Very centrally located – all amenities very accessible.
Parking	Limited on-street parking (eight spaces) is provided. The co-op decides how they should be allocated. This is determined by residents' access requirements. For example, large families with children will probably be prioritised.
Tenure	Social rented (co-operative). The tenant community (650 applied) includes large families, childless couples, pensioners, people with disabilities, single parent families, and key workers.
Uses	Residential and co-op office on ground floor of apartment building.
Building types	Houses and apartment buildings.
Building heights	Nine-storey tower, four-storey apartment buildings, and three-storey houses.
Unit types	Houses and apartments.
Circulation	Each house has its own entrance off the street. Apartments are accessed via circulation cores. There are two lifts in the tower.
Disabled access	All houses have disabled access (ramp up to front doors). Three wheelchair accessible ground floor apartments are available.
Refuse disposal	Houses have a bin area outside the front door. The apartment buildings have their own small garden and bin store.

Communal open space	The development overlooks Bernie Spain Gardens which are for public use.
Private/semi-private open space	Gardens and balconies for houses, balconies for apartments.
Energy saving measures	Passive measures: bigger windows on west facade. Flexibility in house design to allow for future changes.
Management and maintenance	The building has had only one external painting in 5 years. Materials that 'age gracefully' were used. Once completed the scheme was taken over by a separate housing co-operative, called Palm Co-op, which manages the property. All adult residents are members of the co-operative. CSCB also pay a lot of attention to the management of the public realm and community facilities in the Coin Street area. It has set up its own dedicated management team to look after the non-residential parts of its estates. This team ensures that the parks and riverside walkway are maintained in excellent condition for residents, staff of local businesses, and visitors.

THE DESIGN AGENDA

Making connections

Palm Housing sits in a river context that has been 'opened up' so that more people can access and enjoy the Thames in central London. Between 1984 and 1988 CSCB demolished derelict buildings, completed the South Bank riverside walkway and laid out a new riverside park called Bernie Spain Gardens (named after one of the original Coin Street Action Group campaigners). The housing fronts onto this park which also serves as an important public pedestrian route to the river.

The Palm Housing site is extremely well connected. It forms its own narrow urban block, bounded by streets on three sides and the public park on the other. The building reinforces this activity, and movement around its edges by framing and fronting onto the respective spaces.

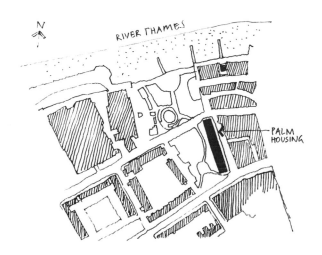

Above   Highly connected routes
around the site
Right   The South Bank context

Providing green areas and corridors

The houses and flats enjoy a very compatible and reciprocal relationship with Bernie Spain Gardens, which link the development to the river. Although the park is public, it provides an attractive outlook for the homes, and the homes provide surveillance over the park.

Housing overlooking Bernie Spain Gardens

Treating the street as a place

As well as providing green links to the river the South Bank has also been the focus of an urban design initiative to improve pedestrian and public transport, and to give the South Bank a more coherent image. The new 'spine route' which has transformed what was once a service route and rat-run into a boulevard with wide pavements and distinctive lighting and street furniture runs past the south end of the Palm Housing development. Broadwall, the street bordered by the housing, accommodates a bus route but is perceived as a street for all users, with decent sized pavements and landscaping, and the parking does not dominate.

A pleasant street environment created on Broadwall

135

Arranging the built form

The site is narrow, long, and constricted, bordered on the east by Broadwall, a street running north to south between Upper Ground and Stamford Street, and on the west by Bernie Spain Gardens. To achieve the required densities, the built form had to cover the bulk of the site, generating a long strip of building accessed from the street. The narrowness of the site forced the architects to consider the interfaces between the building and the public realm surrounding it – often issues that are paid much less attention than necessary. One of the successes of the scheme was the decision to set the building back from the street to create a 'privacy layer' between the street and the building. This important move allows the building to sit comfortably between two important public spaces, with a narrow belt of interface that maintains privacy but does not compromise surveillance and activity.

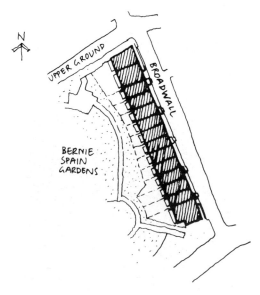

Built form arrangement

Defining public and private space

The fundamental design solution was for the houses and apartment buildings to be entered from the street and to overlook the park. This seems an obvious choice but one which is potentially problematic if executed with a conventional attitude towards fronts and backs of buildings This kind of attitude could have led to either the façade facing the street being like a back entrance, or the façade and private spaces facing the gardens being obvious 'back' spaces. This scheme is an exemplary example of how to deal with public and private space when there is not enough site depth to use the perimeter block device.

The more recent Coin Street project, Iroko, completed in 2002, has the site area and shape to allow a traditional perimeter block form to sit comfortably on the site. The more challenged Palm Housing has two public faces (or two 'fronts') and each is addressed appropriately.

Above Street frontage
Right   Park frontage

Responding to context – scale and massing

With the brief calling for houses and flats, an obvious decision may have been to spread the flats over the top of the houses, to get an even urban scale throughout the scheme. However, the architect's decision was to concentrate the flats in a small tower at the north end of the site, giving good views and signalling the building from the river. This left the remaining accommodation to be arranged as three-storey houses between two four-storey blocks of flats. This varied building scale has a drama that befits its location, and mediates between the public park on one side and the high-rise blocks on the other. To maintain the urban scale of the houses, their third-storey sits below a generous roof void, raised above the normal level to create a double volume space.

The community and council were against the idea of the tower in the beginning, from the point of view of bad associations with high-rise housing, and a general resistance to another tower in the area. A compromise was reached whereby the eleven-storey tower initially proposed was reduced to nine storeys once the clients were convinced that this kind of accommodation with good access and generous balconies, and excellent views would be very attractive for childless couples and single individuals.

The tower has been the key massing success of the scheme – it is an integral part of the scheme's balance, imparting an essential urban scale to the scheme while maintaining the equally essential intimacy and fine grain of a housing scheme. Its slenderness is a factor of its success, owed to each floor only accommodating one apartment. This solution of course is not a common or cost-effective one, but it allowed the tower its pleasing proportion.

Right   *Original competition scheme in*
        the South Bank context
Below *Massing of the final scheme*

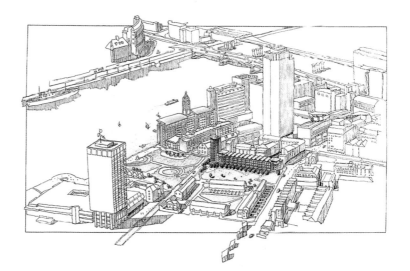

Maximising good aspect and orientating activity to the public realm

The houses are designed so that living spaces are on the west side, overlooking the park, and bedrooms are on the street side, both generating enough activity to interface with the public realm. Stairs and bathrooms are grouped in the centre of the houses, giving over the full width of both 5 m frontages to habitable rooms – bedrooms and living rooms. This allowed the architects to make a feature of both aspects, with activity on both, ensuring surveillance of the street as well as the park.

The park facades are imbued with activity not only through the architectural expression but also the large areas of glazing and generous balconies. This façade also receives full benefit of the sun at all times of the year.

Left   Bedrooms on the street side
Above   Living spaces on the park side

Building in flexibility

The architects' success at overcoming the building layout challenges was met by their understanding of the requirements of the tenants, and how family sizes will change over the years requiring flexible home planning. Through consultation with residents, the architects adopted an approach of designing the houses to be inherently flexible and easy to adapt to changing family needs. The repeated house plan has a band in the middle for stairs and bathrooms. This allowed spaces on either side to become single or twin rooms as desired, a feature that also accommodated habitable rooms on both faces of the building. Living rooms can be at ground, first or second floor levels, and generous lofts allow for further adaptation of the space. The architects produced a series of diagrams illustrating how the houses could be adapted with relative ease to accept virtually any circumstance.

Diagrams showed how dwelling spaces could be used

ALTERNATIVE 1

Responding to context – form and expression

The context of the building poses an interesting issue, one which faces many regeneration or brownfield developments today: the South Bank is distinctly lacking in any particular character or identity. Its undistinguished urban backdrop consists of giant office blocks to the east and the monumental National Theatre to the west. Added to this challenging context, the community wanted something more varied, a richer architecture than the usual social housing solutions.

The response to this was a building with a varied palette of materials (glass, brick, copper, lead, and iroko) contrasting with the monochrome National Theatre and other adjacent developments along the south bank. The building's primary material is red brick, including it in the Oxo Tower and adjacent warehousing family. However, the unique use of timber and glass in both elevations and particularly the park elevation, imbues the building with its own distinct identity. The houses are tall and slim with steeply pitched roofs articulating each house as its own entity within the terrace. The carefully modelled exteriors express the robustly urban street side (entrance) and the more open and animated park side. While providing community housing, the scheme still has a presence appropriate to such a metropolitan site.

The urban context

Meeting the ground – thresholds and interfaces

Because the street front of the building faces onto the backs of warehouses, the architects shifted the terrace back to create an interface zone which was carefully manipulated. This gesture caused the private gardens on the other side to be shallower but this had a positive effect on the interface with the park.

Interface zone between building and pavement

The relationship of the terrace to the street is particularly well handled. The problems of privacy and security that are often associated with house entrances directly on the street are overcome here with the introduction of a secondary raised pavement alongside the building. This raised pavement is ramped at either end to facilitate disabled access to the houses and apartments, but it also performs the function of a buffer zone that need only be used by residents of the buildings. The interface between the raised pavement and the street is mediated with a series of individual steps passing between meter and dustbin enclosures – an elegant solution which makes full use of the often unsightly bin arrangements to subtly define the space on the raised pavement. This space is just big enough to turn a wheelchair, chat with neighbours, or personalise the space with some individual touch. This subtle transition from public space to semi-private space to private space within the home is a model for this kind of urban scenario.

Managing privacy and surveillance

The gardens for each house are relatively shallow and are overlooked by the balconies above. The gardens meet the adjacent park with a brick wall, the quality detailing of which prevents it from looking like a back garden wall, which is obviously critical considering its public interface. The success of the design of this wall is the fact that it provides privacy for the gardens but in a positive way – the wall is an attractive element of the scheme and is low and visually permeable enough to create a decent edge to the park that does not alienate its users. This is helped by the fact that the houses overlook the park, making it feel entirely safe at all times of the day.

The privacy of the gardens is maintained despite the relatively low screen wall as the private gardens are at a slightly lower level than the public gardens. This level change is a model method of providing privacy without having to resort to eye-level blank walls. Supplementing this device is the planting between the wall and Bernie Spain gardens, creating a buffer zone that prevents people from peering directly into the private gardens.

Small gardens create an interface between building and park

SUMMARY OF SUCCESSES

- *The built form arrangement provides two active frontages along a challengingly narrow site.*

- *The massing creates drama and interest on an urban scale while maintaining residential intimacy through a fine grain building expression.*

- *Interfaces between the building and the public spaces are well designed to maintain privacy for the homes and surveillance of the public spaces.*

- *The building enjoys a positive relationship with the public gardens, providing good aspect for the homes, and an attractive and active edge to the park.*

- *Plans allow flexibility in layout to accommodate changing family needs.*

11

HOMES IN THE CALLE DEL CARME

Barcelona, Spain

Architect
Josep Llinas Carmona
Developer/client
Procivesa
Completed
1995

A project that integrally serves the needs of the dwellings and the street. No design decisions compromise one for the other.

This is an urban project that is highly tuned to its context – contrasting with and complementing the immediate area, responding to the challenges of urban infill with skill and a real understanding of how urban spaces work. The architect has manipulated the brief and built form to make the building and its context legible to users.

BACKGROUND

In the historic centre of Barcelona, the district known as the Barrio del Raval has undergone several regeneration initiatives. The dense fabric of rundown houses is the context for this project, which has seemingly acted as a catalyst for further projects and which has certainly uplifted the immediate area. The plot became available following the demolition of several houses which faced a narrow dark lane, the Calle d'En Roig – a street of medieval dimensions, 4 m wide and 140 m long. The plot is on the corner of this lane and a lively shopping street, the Calle del Carme, a couple of minutes' walk from Las Ramblas.

UP FRONT

Number of dwellings	28.
Site area	Approximately 0.68 ha.
Density	Approximately 411 dph.
Access to public transport	Central location served by good public transport.
Access to amenities	Central location – shopping streets very close by, most facilities very accessible.
Parking	Basement parking accessed from the street.
Tenure	Private.
Uses	Residential with commercial premises on the ground floor.
Building types	Apartment building.
Building heights	Five or six storeys.
Unit types	Apartments.
Circulation	Three circulation cores serve two or three apartments per floor.
Disabled access	Lifts to all units.
Communal open space	None.
Private/semi-private open space	Apartments on the first floor have terraces.

THE DESIGN AGENDA

Making connections

The project sits within a highly permeable historic street pattern. Its main contribution to the existing movement pattern is that it improves its quality and legibility. The building realigns the street to make more of a connection with the Calle del Carme.

Left Position and extent of the site in the street network

Above Building on the corner of the two streets

Laying out the built form

The municipal planning requirements permitted total coverage of the site. However, the difficulties of a 50 m long continuous building, 15 or 16 m high, fronting onto a street only 4 m wide, were soon recognised. The problems were not only about the quality of the buildings but also about the quality of the narrow street. A continuous façade would lose the opportunity to do something about the starkness of the Calle d'En Roig. The response to this challenge was two fold: to deflect the building form inwards towards the centre of the site, giving the street more light and space, and to create three separate buildings at the upper level to allow sunlight to pass between them and improve the sombre Calle Roig environment.

The skill in arranging the built form in detail on this narrow site was in its horizontal layering – the plans at ground, first and upper levels are all different, with a very fine grain contextual response at each level. The plan at the ground floor splays out to the Calle del Carme which is a busier shopping street. This opens up the canyon of the street in a funnel shape towards Calle del Carme, inviting some of the activity into the narrower street. The first floor level follows the previous line of built form most closely, while on the upper floors the building dissolves into three pavilions which read as free-standing elements.

The first building on the corner realigns with the original street opening, expressed as a projection. The second, in the middle, is withdrawn from the building edge and is barely visible from the street. The third, at the far end of the site, reinforces the new alignment of the street.

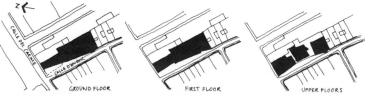

Above *View towards the Calle del Carme along Carrer d'En Roig*
Right *Varying ground, first and upper floor plans*

Treating the street as a place

The almost 50 m long building front gave the opportunity to increase the quality of the street as a social place. The generous height of the ground floor gives the street a sense of enclosure along the new alignment. This allows the upper blocks to dislodge from the street alignment without the coherence of the street being compromised. Dislodging these upper buildings allowed more light into the street.

Left   *View along Carrer d'En Roig beyond the building*
Right   *The street edge is realigned to improve pedestrian space*

Orienting active fronts to the public realm

In this project a fine balance had to be struck between providing activity to the street, and protecting the privacy of the residents and their neighbours. Living rooms were placed on the corners of the three pavilions, directing the views from these rooms up and down the street instead of directly across the street.

On the ground floor three commercial spaces have a direct relationship with the street, taking advantage of the active corner location.

Above Commercial units facing the street
Right Living rooms are placed on corners

Providing frequent and convenient access

Despite the spatial constraints on the site, the architect provided three separate circulation cores, each accessing two or three apartments per floor. This was necessary to generate the three separate 'blocks' at the upper levels, but was also very beneficial to the street environment in terms of the extra activity generated by the entrances. Having three separate circulation cores also allowed more privacy, personalisation and control over the common parts by the few apartments using each core.

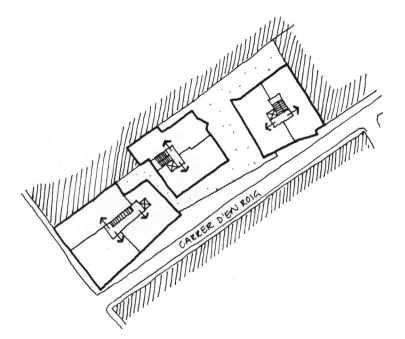

Each block has its own circulation core

Maximising solar potential, aspect and privacy

The building form has been cleverly manipulated to gain light into the apartments by introducing gaps between the buildings and by pulling them away from the edge of the streets to varying degrees. However, the spaces between the buildings are very small and the protection of privacy from one apartment to another is an issue. Windows have been carefully placed to minimise privacy conflicts.

Above   Maximising good light and aspect
Right   Maximising good light and aspect

Managing parking

The entrance to the basement parking, which has a solid gate, is directly off the street. This gate is at the far end of the elevation and does not have a negative impact on the street frontage. The only clue that it is access to the basement is when cars approach and the gate swings open. The circulation cores go down into the basement so that apartments can be accessed directly. As in many streets in Barcelona, graffiti has made its way onto the garage doors. While in many cases this would be a symptom of streets or spaces that have no surveillance over them, in this case the presence of graffiti here is mainly attributed to the fact that the solid surface of the door is available.

Discreet entrance to basement parking

Spaces around the home

In this high-density situation, it was only the first floor apartments that were given formal terraces, using the roof of the commercial premises below. There were still privacy issues to be dealt with, resulting in the shuttered screen between the terraces and the street. The other apartments do not have formal semi-private spaces. However, the tradition of using shutters on all the windows for shading is also very useful for extending spaces outside. Shutters can be opened at any angle, to provide shade or privacy, or allow maximum daylighting when completely open. When slightly ajar, they create a zone of extra space that extends outwards from the apartment. This has been maximised by setting the line of windows to the inside of the reveal, increasing the perceived 'outdoor' space, and by providing a horizontal rail or balustrade to encourage the use of the space.

Above Windows set back to create a semi-private space
Right Shuttered screen gives privacy to terraces on the first floor

157

Responding to the context – expression

The building brings light, freshness and grace to the street which is generally characterised by plaster and stone façades. However, it still maintains the character of the street, complementing it with a new element of variety. The street is distinguished from the other similar narrow dark streets by its new entrance from the Calle del Carme. The street's new character is also attributed to the light that illuminates the buildings.

The inventive corner treatment gives a new character and scale to the entrance of the lane. The corner building echoes the historic alignment of the street at the upper levels. At the ground level it is hollowed out to signal the widening of the lane and the meeting of the two streets.

Both streets are enlivened and the volumes and treatment of the new are manipulated to reconcile with the scale and texture of the existing.

Left   Responding to local context
Above   Corner treatment

SUMMARY OF SUCCESSES

- *The design of this development considered the environmental quality of the street as much as that of the apartments.*

- *Skilful design limited the conflicts of privacy between the apartments in the development and across the street.*

- *The building mass is broken down in a series of layers – a fine grain response to allow light into the apartments and into the street.*

- *A fresh expression that complements and adds variety to the historic district.*

Conclusion

Front to back

Slowly but surely we are getting it right. At both ends of the urban scale, from visionary masterplans to intricate inner city infill projects, the real issues of what makes good places are being addressed. What we know is that it is not easy: with all the pressures of modern day development, design professionals are faced with more challenges than ever. But we are also discovering that it does not cost more, or compromise much, to start seeing buildings, spaces and people as inseparable elements of a complex matrix. To do this, and get urban housing the right way round, means thinking beyond the building box. And this can only enrich the design process and product.

This book has promoted a design-led approach to housing. It has suggested an agenda of design issues for urban housing, within a frame of reference that encompasses broad urban design objectives; environmental sustainability; the engagement of communities in the design process; and the important social values and socio-spatial qualities that drive our decisions. The design agenda has been put forward as a useful tool for designers, to direct the design process, to explain a scheme, or to use it as a mechanism for reviewing or examining a project.

In the second half of the book, the design agenda has been used to review the selected case studies. Out of this investigation one could suggest two broad conclusions.

- Firstly, the projects are all very successful, but for different reasons. Their success is often attributed to decisions that seem to contradict some basic 'rules' about how to make successful places. Indeed, it has become clear that it is these idiosyncratic decisions that makes the built environment richer, but they are based on achieving a certain environmental quality, rather than being the result of ignorance or a lack of true understanding of the issues.

- Secondly, and fundamentally, what all the projects do have in common is that they display a positive relationship between the buildings and the spaces between and around them. In each case, the scheme is not a piece of architecture that stands alone as an object: to varying degrees, each scheme takes design to the urban scale, looking beyond the buildings, to the context and the spaces, and the way people interact with them. Social processes and the physical form of the urban environment have not been viewed in isolation.

Lessons have also been learnt. Most of the projects have tackled one or more tricky issues, many of which are becoming generic design challenges for urban housing. The projects display various degrees of success, and their lack of full resolution in some areas could be attributed to many external factors that overwhelm design considerations. However, the discussion around these emerging issues can be surmised as follows.

Public and private (fronts and backs)

It has been proved and shown that there is nothing wrong with high density, and the move towards urban living is slowly gaining currency and support. What we usually do not see in the glossy advertisements for new urban residential developments is how the buildings are laid out with respect to each other and their context (streets and neighbouring properties), how public and private space is arranged, and how people move from one space to another. The message about high density needs to be more than the fact that urban living is sustainable. The success of high-density housing is very dependant on high quality urban design, with particular emphasis on the relationship between buildings and spaces. All the case studies we have seen yield good densities, appropriate for their urban settings. But it is not their density alone that makes them special. It is the way the buildings and spaces enjoy a happy symbiosis, the key design factor in making higher densities work. There are many reasons why so many post war estates in the UK are being pulled down, but a central reason in design terms is the lack of ownership, definition, and quality of the space between and around buildings. The tower block raised on pilotis in a sea of space is a case in point.

Making clear distinctions between public and private space is a key consideration. In most of the case studies this distinction and the appropriate orientation of fronts and backs is a measure of the project's success. Generally, building fronts face public space, and building backs face private space. This rule can be broken without too much compromise, but it usually relies on external resources.

Century Court is an example: the main terrace of apartments is accessed from the court (the 'back' side of the building), while the terrace of houses is accessed from the street on the other side of the development (the 'front' side of the building).

This has meant that in the central court, there is an interface between the backs of the houses and the front entrances of the apartments. The court is a less positive space than it could have been, presented on one side by a long line of blank back garden fences. But the high landscape quality of the courtyard space is forgiving. In schemes with less access to funding for maintenance, management and good landscaping, and without the security and exclusivity of projects like Century Court, these kinds of interfaces should be avoided.

Grids and permeability

If we look back at all the case studies, we see that they all sit within or generate a permeable movement network of some form or another. We have seen the strictly orthogonal grid of Parc de Bercy, which responds to the formality of the park; the organic but equally permeable grid of Bo01 in Malmo; the reinforcement and enhancement of existing movement patterns at Century Court, Coin Street, and in the Barcelona scheme. We have also seen that permeability is not enough on its own. Permeability is a buzzword, there is pressure for projects to have that box ticked. But what we do not want is a series of pedestrian paths that provide plenty of linkages but which are not attractive and safe routes in themselves. In each of the case studies permeability has been complemented by buildings aligning and overlooking the paths or streets – there are no arbitrary pedestrian footpaths making connections through undefined and unfriendly spaces. Routes should not be added as a separate layer to a scheme – the movement network, as suggested in the design agenda, is a primary design decision to be made, and the form should then follow, framing and channelling the movement.

The new Bo01 neighbourhood has many pedestrian connections that run along the backs of properties or through spaces relatively undefined by buildings. This kind of permeability is not negative here because of the extremely high-quality landscaping and treatment of the public realm. However, if it is to be used as a model, the necessary structures for management and maintenance of the various spaces must be in place. This of course becomes an expense for residents. In projects which are less exclusive, and with less access to such financial resources, it is more beneficial to make sure that the routes and spaces are safe and attractive by considering their relationship with the buildings more carefully. Quality landscaping can then be a bonus, not an absolute requirement.

Development parcels

An issue that is not often discussed but which is raised when comparing masterplans like Bo01 to Parc de Bercy, is how residential quality is impacted on by the way masterplans are divided up into various development parcels. This is an issue that presents itself whenever a masterplan is to be built out by a number of developers and architects. This scenario in itself is positive as it encourages variety, but the way in which it is done deserves more attention.

Bo01 was divided up by blocks or plots, each development parcel standing alone, and bordered by public streets and spaces. With the lack of any form of design coding, the result is interesting and varied, but also lacks a certain urban coherence. In many cases a street or space is bordered by two radically different architectural expressions, which often appear to be competitive rather than complementary. This is not a big problem at Bo01 as the landscape and public realm quality is so high that the streets and spaces function as a legible framework holding it all together. This of course depends on management, maintenance and deep pockets.

In contrast, Parc de Berry had a more rigorous design framework and this was complemented by a development parcelling strategy where plots were not divided by streets but rather straddled them. This meant that buildings on either side of a street were designed by the same architect, putting a lot of emphasis on the quality of the street itself. This approach generated a strong legibility in the public realm that was not dependant on high-quality landscaping. However, the result could also be perceived as being slightly bland. The ideal, perhaps, is somewhere in the middle — a balance that satisfies both variety and urban coherence.

Century Court demonstrates the variety that can be achieved on a given site in an existing street network. This is a fine example of how a development need not look like the work of one architect, even if it is. This kind of variety within a scheme is not arbitrary, it comes out of responding to each edge or contextual condition in an appropriate and different way. The fact that it comes from one architect gives the overall scheme a necessary coherence.

Parking

While high-density urban housing depends on good quality buildings and spaces, it also presents important design challenges in how to accommodate parking so that it does not impact on the amenity of residents. In sustainability terms the arrangement at Palm Housing in Coin Street is the most positive: the housing is so centrally located that the need for cars is limited and reduced parking levels can easily be justified. The parking that is provided is accommodated on the street, contributing to activity in the street without dominating it with cars. Of course, attractive as this scenario is, it is not always easy to achieve.

The parking arrangement at Century Court in Cheltenham represents the other end of the scale. The parking requirement was reduced relative to normal standards for that kind of housing offer, which was very positive and necessary for this high-density scheme to be deliverable. However, the demand was still high enough to necessitate a basement for parking. Basements, while costly, are the most positive way of accommodating this scale of parking as they allow the spaces between buildings to be dedicated to amenity spaces. Access to the basements is important, however. In the case of Century Court, the ramps going down into the basement tend to break up a potentially very attractive and cohesive amenity space.

Most parking solutions will fall somewhere between these two scenarios – probably where there is less justification for reduced parking, and/or where the funding for basement parking is not available. Whether the solutions are to accommodate cars in the streets, parking courts or under the buildings, the challenge is to minimise the impact of cars on people and the landscape.

Living above the shop

Incorporating other uses in a housing scheme is an aspiration of most designers – we all know the benefits of mixed-use development, the activity and variety it can bring to a neighbourhood. But most of the time it is not easy to achieve. Often the market demand for alternative uses only arises some time after the project has been completed, or when the critical mass of residents is large enough to support new shops or community facilities. It seems then that we face more of a challenge in designing for flexibility than in slavishly getting non-residential uses in our buildings from the outset. Rather than have empty shops, perhaps it is better to have spaces that can adapt as market needs change.

The Tango scheme in Malmo does this very well. Its ground floor apartments facing the canal-side street can easily be changed into commercial units with their own access directly off the street. The housing in Barcelona was designed specifically for commercial uses on the ground floor, not just to achieve the desired use mix, but also to avoid the privacy problems that come with ground floor dwellings on such narrow streets. Nearly 10 years after the project's completion these commercial units are doing well, but probably owe a lot of their success to the incremental regeneration of the area over the years. The model for the Parc de Bercy housing is that all the apartments are above ground floor level, with other uses occupying the ground floor. This concept is very beneficial for protecting the privacy of the dwellings and affording them good views over the park, but it leaves the ground floor slightly bereft of activity, as many of the commercial units are unoccupied.

The decision to allocate the entire ground floor along the park to other uses was perhaps a bit too optimistic, especially seeing that the local high street runs along the other side of the housing.

Let's dance

The principles and design issues discussed in this book apply at all levels of design. In some cases they are more focused on finer, more detailed design decisions; that is, where the site is smaller and more constrained, Palm Housing in London, or the housing in Barcelona for example. In other cases like Bo01 in Malmo and Parc de Bercy in Paris, there has been scope in the scale of the masterplanning project to make strategic decisions like setting out movement networks and block structures.

Good design does not depend on the scale of the project – the same principles have to apply across all design scales. From the design of street networks to the arrangement of rooms and windows in an apartment the aspiration is the same – to make sure that the street is well defined, the building aligns and overlooks the street, privacy is maintained etc. These considerations have to be addressed over and over again, as design decisions become more and more detailed.

The case studies have amply demonstrated that quality can be realised in many different ways. They do by no means represent all the eventualities and contextual challenges that may arise, and in their diversity they represent the fact that universal rules for good housing design cannot apply. What this handful of diverse examples does show is how varied responses might be, while all still satisfying the needs of urban living. Good housing is not the product of a set of design rules; it is not about knowing what to do and what not to do and applying these rules indiscriminately. It is about understanding how we want our housing projects to perform, at all scales: city, neighbourhood and individual homes. It is about using this knowledge and responding afresh to every new site with all its opportunities and challenges. It is about getting the approach right.

Right at the beginning of this book, it was suggested that if we started thinking about backs and fronts more carefully, we may be on the way to making places rather than buildings. Place-making is about relationships. The mere fact that we refer to our building elevations as facades implies that they face something, they have a relationship with something, and that something is not a camera, it is usually a space or building with a person in it. What we have seen here is a handful of housing projects that boast sound relationships between buildings and spaces. The projects are not only about the dancers but also the choreography. No wonder they perform so well.

References and
further reading

Alexander, C., Ishikawa, S., Silverstein, M. *et al.* (1977) *A Pattern Language*, New York: Oxford University Press.

Bentley, I. (1999) *Urban Transformations*, London: Routledge.

Bentley, I., Alcock, A., Murrain, P. *et al.* (1985) *Responsive Environments: A Manual for Designers*, Oxford: Architectural Press.

Bullivant, L. (2003) *AD Home Front: New Developments in Housing*, England: John Wiley & Sons Ltd.

Calvino, I. (1997) *Invisible Cities*, London: Random House.

Colquloun, I. (1999) *RIBA Book of Twentieth Century British Housing*, Oxford: Architectural Press.

DETR, RIBA, RTPI & NHBC (1997–2004) *Home A Place to Live: Housing Design Awards*, Birmingham, Housing Design Awards Office.

DTLR/Cabe (2001) *Better Places to Live: By Design*, London: Thomas Telford Publishing.

Edwards, B. and Turrent, D. (2000) *Sustainable Housing*, London: Spon Press.

English Partnerships and the Housing Corporation (2000) *Urban Design Compendium*, London: English Partnerships.

Garnham, T. (2004) *Lines on the Landscape, Circles from the Sky*, Stroud, Gloucestershire: Tempus.

Gehl, J. (1987) *Life Between Buildings*, New York: Van Nostrand Reinhold.

Greater London Authority (2003) *Housing for a Compact City*, London: Greater London Authority.

Hayward, R. and McGlynn, S. (1993) *Making Better Places*, Oxford: Butterworth.

Jacobs, J. (1961) *The Death and Life of Great American Cities*, New York: Random House.

Katz, P. (1994) *The New Urbanism: Toward an Architecture of Community*, New York: McGraw-Hill, Inc.

More, T. (1965) *The Complete Works of St. Thomas More. Volume 4: Utopia*, New Haven: Yale University Press.

Rudlin, D. and Falk, N. (1999) *Building the 21st Century Home: The Sustainable Urban Neighbourhood*, Oxford: Architectural Press.

Thomas, R. (Ed) (2003) *Sustainable Urban Design: An Environmental Approach*, London: Spon Press.

Sennet, R. (1993) *The Fall of Public Man*, London: Faber and Faber Ltd.

Sherlock, H. (1991) *Cities are Good for Us*, London: Paladin.

Urban Task Force (1999) *Towards an Urban Renaissance*, London: E&FN Spon.

Further information on case studies

Tango Housing, Bo01, Malmo
Architectural Record, Vol. 190, No. 2, Feb 2002, pp. 149–166
and www.ekostaden.com

Housing at Parc de Bercy
Architecture d'Aujourd'hui, Vol. 295, Oct 1994, pp. 57–101

Century Court, Cheltenham
RIBA Journal, Vol. 108, No. 6, June 2001, pp. 32–38
and www.cabe.org.uk/library

Palm Housing, Coin Street, London
Architecture Today, Vol. 52, Oct 1994, pp. 40–48
and www.coinstreet.org

Homes at Calle del Carme, Barcelona
Arquitectura Viva, Vol. 50, Sept–Oct 1996, pp. 104–107

Illustrations
acknowledgements

The author and publishers would like to thank the following individuals and organisations for permission to reproduce material. All other photographs and illustrations by Sally Lewis.

Chapter 3

Chapter 5

Index